The College Writer's Guide to the Study of Literature

The College Writer's Guide to the Study of Literature

Christopher R. Reaske
THE UNIVERSITY OF MICHIGAN

Library of Congress Catalog Card Number: 71-97839

Manufactured in the United States of America.

DESIGNED BY ANDREW ZUTIS

FIRST PRINTING

Acknowledgments

I am particularly grateful to Northrop Frye, consulting reader, for reading my manuscript and making helpful suggestions, and to John Rodenbeck for answering numerous questions. From Random House, I received continuing support and help from James B. Smith, and excellent editorial assistance in preparing the final manuscript from June Fischbein.

Acknowledgment is gratefully made to the following authors and publishers:

W. H. Auden, "The Unknown Citizen" from *The Collected Poetry of W. H. Auden.* Copyright 1940 by W. H. Auden. By permission of Random House, Inc., and Faber and Faber, Ltd.

Robert Bridges, "London Snow" from *Collected Poems of Robert Bridges.* By permission of The Clarendon Press, Oxford.

Stephen Crane, "War Is Kind" from *Collected Poems.* By permission of Alfred A. Knopf, Inc.

Adelaide Crapsey, "The Lonely Death" from *Verse.* Copyright 1922 and renewed 1950 by the Adelaide Crapsey Foundation. By permission of Alfred A. Knopf, Inc.

Emily Dickinson, "I Died for Beauty" and "There's a Certain Slant of Light" from *The Complete Poems of Emily Dickinson,* edited by Thomas H. Johnson. By permission of Little, Brown and Company.

T. S. Eliot, "The Love Song of J. Alfred Prufrock" from *Collected Poems, 1909–1962. Murder in the Cathedral* from *The Complete Poems and Plays, 1909–1950.* By permission of Harcourt, Brace & World, Inc., and Faber and Faber, Ltd.

John Gould Fletcher, "Like Snowballs Tossed" from *Collected Poems.* By permission of Houghton Mifflin Company.

Robert Frost, "Fire and Ice," "The Pasture," and "The Road Not Taken" from *Complete Poems of Robert Frost.* Copyright 1916,

For

Mary Katharine

Preface

THIS BOOK is designed to introduce college students to the basic methods and terminology conventionally used to write about poetry, drama, and fiction. It adheres to the patterns of thinking and writing about literature which have now more or less been stabilized by the practice of literary criticism.

While focusing on the major genres, I have attempted to call attention to the constant imaginative efforts to break with convention. In this age of free verse, antitheatrical theater, and nonfiction novels, it would be limiting to adhere *exclusively* to any formalistic methodology.

I have tried to write this book in a direct, economical way, and those who might prefer a wittier handling of the material will, I hope, nevertheless benefit from my brevity and feel at least some relief from my efforts to value precision over pontification.

CHRISTOPHER R. REASKE

Ann Arbor, Michigan
February 1969

Contents

The College Writer's Guide to the Study of Literature

PART ONE

Poetry

What Is a Poem?

Writing about poetry will always be an exciting yet imperfect activity, and every critical analysis of a particular poem will be the last but one. In the first place, much of the language used to discuss poetry is slippery and imprecise. Secondly, there are certain things happening in a poem which simply cannot be rearticulated by the reader—and frequently not even by the poet himself. There is a gulf in poetry between inspiration and execution, or between conception and presentation, and while we can talk with some precision about a poem's technical execution, we are, at the outset, sentenced to a certain amount of speculation when considering the soul-like inspiration in the poet's heart and the poem's conception in his mind. This speculation, and the recording of our emotional response, is very exciting. As Anatole France once noted, "the good critic is he who narrates the adventures of his soul among masterpieces."

While there are certain intangible feelings in a poem, there is also a technical shape about it which we can carefully describe by using certain fundamental terms which literary analysis has now more or less stabilized. The materials of poetry are of two kinds, then, conventionally grouped as experience and form, or as content and technique (Mark Schorer's division). With regard to form or technique, the student of literature, like the poet himself, has available a substantial number of tools, and it is with these that the college student who wants to write about literature should begin. It is necessary to point out, however, that a poem does not need to *be* at all in any technical sense. Anyone may scribble a few random words and call them "my poem." The world indulges self-definitions, particularly in the arts. Andy Warhol's famous silkscreen of stacks of Campbell's Tomato Soup cans, *he* says, is art. We can consider it good art or bad art as our personal taste dictates, but in any case we are willing to talk about it as *art of some kind*. The same holds true for poetry.

In analyzing a poem we need to begin by describing its physical features—rhyme, length, meter, poetic devices, etc., and then proceed to an explication of its meaning and a critical evaluation of its effectiveness and artistry in communicating that meaning. It is important to remember that we are separating the more concrete features of poetry from the more abstract features only for purposes of discussion, not because the two kinds of features actually exist independently.

What Does a Poem Do?

Poetry does different things for different readers. Some respond with emotion—sadness, joy, love, sorrow, etc.—some respond only with thought, hunting immediately for the "message" or central meaning of the poem. Some prefer the intellectual gamesmanship of ferreting out peripheral meanings and recondite implications. It seems logical to agree at the outset that what a poem does, in the most basic sense, is to say something. That may, at first, sound simplistic, but it is nevertheless probably the best summary of what a poem does. A poet writes a poem because he has something he wants to say, something he wants to put into words. As T. S. Eliot wrote, "I gotta use words when I talk to you." The poet usually writes with a reader in mind, and even Emily Dickinson (1830–1886), who purportedly never wanted anyone to read her curious, brilliant poems, kept them neatly tied in little bundles in her bureau drawer where they were easily "discovered."

Literature as an art form began as both entertainment and instruction. The double role of poetry has always been to teach and delight. Horace, who was concerned with the complexities of aesthetic experience, compared poetry to pictures and suggested that both can be superficially arresting or densely compact. A poem may speak to us in iambic tetrameter or trochaic dimeter, or in no metrical pattern at all. The point is that it *does* speak to us, does try to tell us something, sometimes something very abstract. We find in a poem, then, both a subject matter (theme) and an idea or point of view about that subject matter.

Subject Matter or Theme

The subject matter is usually referred to as the theme. For example, we discuss the theme of temptation in Milton's *Paradise Lost* or the theme of personal alienation in Robinson's "Richard Cory." Consider the following poem by Stephen Crane (1871–1900):

WAR IS KIND

Do not weep maiden, for war is kind.
Because your lover threw wild hands toward the sky
And the affrighted steed ran on alone,
Do not weep.
War is kind.

Hoarse, booming drums of the regiment,
Little souls who thirst for fight,
These men were born to drill and die.
The unexplained glory flies above them,
Great is the battle-god, great, and his kingdom—
A field where a thousand corpses lie.

Do not weep, babe, for war is kind.
Because your father tumbled in the yellow trenches,
Raged at his breast, gulped and died,
Do not weep.
War is kind.

Swift blazing flag of the regiment,
Eagle with crest of red and gold,
These men were born to drill and die.
Point for them the virtue of slaughter,
Make plain to them the excellence of killing
And a field where a thousand corpses lie.

Mother whose heart hung humble as a button
On the bright splendid shroud of your son,
Do not weep.
War is kind.

The subject matter, or theme, of Crane's poem is war. Crane makes the poem universal—that is, about war at all times and in all places—by introducing basic patterns of human emotion—the maiden weeping for a dead lover, a baby weeping for a dead father, a mother weeping for a dead son. The deaths of men in battle consistently generate these emotions. What the poem "says" is that war is horrible. Literally, Crane keeps repeating "War is kind," that is, he uses *irony*, or dissimulation, saying the opposite of what is true in order to make the truth more vital and dramatic. Each time he says "War is kind," we find ourselves saying, "no, it is not kind, it is hideous." This is the way Crane *wants* us to read what he is writing. In other words, while we talk about the fact that a poem says something, we need to be careful that we understand what is meant, not simply what is literally written. Crane's poem "tells us" that war is a horrible feature of reality which creates immeasurable sadness in all sections and strata of society. Furthermore, Crane deftly disputes the idea that men, through some strange kind of grotesque vanity, love fighting for glory: the soldiers of Crane's experience are born, trained for meaningless wars, and then die in battle without the vaguest conception of glory—"The unexplained glory flies above them." The "battle-god," the only one who benefits from war, is death—who, in the end, can survey his "kingdom," a field of corpses.

Didacticism

When poetry tries to teach us something, to instruct us, we refer to it as *didactic poetry*. Usually a moral is being offered, though occasionally we find "didactic" poetry of a different sort—that which conveys specific factual information or even dogma. Poems obviously have different degrees of didacticism, some being emphatically didactic, others only secondarily or incidentally didactic. Crane's poem about war is didactic, because it tries to explain to us that war is futile and cruel; the poem has this particular point of view to express.

There are few poems which do not have a didactic dimension, though in many it is marginal or slight. When a poem says something specifically about life, and about how we should approach life, it is generally teaching us in the same sense that the Greek philosophers may be said to have taught. Behind the teaching is a set of standards which the teacher (poet) hopes the pupil (reader) will adopt. Consider, for example, Robert Frost's dramatic attempt to teach us that it can make an important difference in life if we sometimes do the unconventional thing, make the more pointedly individualistic choice. Extremely didactic verse—that which hits us over the head with moral arguments—has become repugnant to modern taste; but consider the smooth logic of Frost:

THE ROAD NOT TAKEN

Two roads diverged in a yellow wood,
And sorry I could not travel both
And be one traveler, long I stood
And looked down one as far as I could
To where it bent in the undergrowth;

Then took the other, as just as fair,
And having perhaps the better claim,
Because it was grassy and wanted wear;
Though as for that the passing there
Had worn them really about the same.

And both that morning equally lay
In leaves no step had trodden black.
Oh, I kept the first for another day!
Yet knowing how way leads on to way,
I doubted if I should ever come back.

I shall be telling this with a sigh
Somewhere ages and ages hence:
Two roads diverged in a wood, and I—
I took the one less traveled by,
And that has made all the difference.

This poem is not didactic in the sense of trying to persuade us to endorse a particular dogmatic belief, but rather in that it is trying to teach us something about the patterns of life from the perspective of one who is thinking about the pattern of his own life. The speaker intuitively suspects that once he starts down one path rather than the other, it is extremely unlikely that he will ever return and try the other path. Life does not work that way; our voyage through life is a slipping through a series of canal locks, each part opening into the next and so forth. The poem, then, has a kind of quiet fatalism; the speaker is wise enough to realize that for each act of his life there will be unforeseen and yet inevitable consequences. "The Road Not Taken" says that each of our individual actions *will* make a difference in the overall pattern of our life. The poem is also inspirational in its subdued wisdom. It stimulates us into self-inquiry. We find ourselves contemplating the alternatives among which we have had to choose. We find ourselves curiously relieved to know that our individual decisions have made (and, more importantly, will make) significant differences in our lives. In other words, while a poem usually says something and entertains us, it also presents us with something against which we can match or compare our private ideas, beliefs, and opinions. It may be that some readers of "The Road Not Taken" will not easily be led to believe that such decisions do make much difference. Some readers will find Frost's metaphorical crossroads rather simplistic; life, these readers might argue, does not present many "A or B" decisions any more, but rather an enormous intersection of choices (A or B or C or D, etc.). But no matter what the individual reader's reaction to the poem is, it has nevertheless presented something for him to react to, has presented an idea, a concept, a picture, a story, which we consider, reflect on, and then either agree or disagree with.

Emotional Involvement

In addition to saying something, a poem usually excites us in some way. While we make an intellectualized response to what a poem says, we also have an emotional experience when we read a poem. Because we are usually made to experience a change in our feelings, either feeling happier, sadder, more in love, etc., we can write about "how we experience the poem." That is, we can describe our involvement (or our failure to become involved, as the case may be). From this point of view, writing about poetry is similar to telling a friend how we *feel* when we listen to a particular song or kind of music.

No two readers of a poem will be excited in the same way, much less to the same degree. The point is that we need to explain *how* a poem excites us, if it does,, or, perhaps, why it does not excite us. There is a definite relationship between what the poet was doing when he wrote his poem and what we are feeling when we read it. This relationship is not entirely cerebral.

Artistic stimulation assumes a connection between mind and sense, between intellect and emotion. For purposes of discussion, to write about poetry, we sometimes try to separate our emotional response from our intellectual response, but we need to be able to analyze honestly our precise feelings about both a poem's mood and its message. Often, in fact, a poet impresses us more with mood than message. Consider the following well-known poem by Lord Byron (George Noel Gordon, 1788–1824):

SHE WALKS IN BEAUTY

– I –

She walks in beauty, like the night
  Of cloudless climes and starry skies;
And all that's best of dark and bright
  Meet in her aspect and her eyes:
Thus mellowed to that tender light
  Which Heaven to gaudy day denies.

– II –

One shade the more, one ray the less,
  Had half impaired the nameless grace
Which waves in every raven tress,
  Or softly lightens o'er her face;
Where thoughts serenely sweet express
  How pure, how dear their dwelling-place.

– III –

And on that cheek, and o'er that brow,
  So soft, so calm, yet eloquent,
The smiles that win, the tints that glow,
  But tell of days in goodness spent,
A mind at peace with all below,
  A heart whose love is innocent!

Here Byron is capturing the essence of his beloved's perfection. There is no strong message or moral. Everything supports the fundamentally emotional framework established by the speaker's adoration of a beautiful woman. We respond to this poem in an almost purely emotional way. We feel an exhilaration, an excited breathlessness, because we are swept up—involved—in the speaker's (apparent) rapture. When we ask what a poem does, we must always remember that there is the dual role of poetry, to teach and to delight. The two categories are not exclusive; however, our first response to a poem is usually either mainly emotional or mainly intellectual. Our analysis more often than not will follow from that initial reaction. In writing about Byron's poem, we would probably indicate the technical features of the poem, pointing out that it is written in three six-line stanzas (sestets) with a rhyme scheme of *ababab* and a metrical pattern of iambic tetrameter. We would then move, quite swiftly really, into a discussion of the poem as a conventional love poem in which the reader becomes involved in the speaker's expression of his great admiration for a beautiful woman whom he describes with hyperbole. We would discuss our emotional participation in, or experience of, this poem and attempt to indicate our basic feelings of joy, love, and happiness.

As a kind of contrast, consider a short poem by Emily Dickinson:

I DIED FOR BEAUTY

I died for beauty, but was scarce
Adjusted in the tomb,
When one who died for truth was lain
In an adjoining room.

He questioned softly why I failed?
"For beauty," I replied.
"And I for truth—the two are one;
We brethren are," he said.

And so, as kinsmen met a-night,
We talked between the rooms,
Until the moss had reached our lips,
And covered up our names.

Emily Dickinson's poem is so intentionally intellectual, so definitely a "message" poem, that we can hardly respond to it in any other way. Perhaps aware of the Keatsian equation of truth and beauty, we simply say, yes, from the poet's point of view, truth and beauty are the same. The point after this, however, is that both of the characters in this poem are *dead*. The macabre final picture of the moss growing up over their lips distills the full message of the poem—that whether one feels one is serving the cause of beauty or the cause of truth, no matter what idealized name one gives to one's activity, one *does* die. We realize that there is an ironic inversion in the poem because Dickinson has chosen to talk about two people who have died for something, rather than about what these two people lived for (though there is a subtle equation here of course). The pursuit of the ideal (Truth, Beauty) is, ultimately, doomed (note that the speaker is asked why he "failed"). Technically, the poem is written—like Byron's—in three stanzas. But while the meter is consistent—alternation of lines of iambic tetrameter with lines of iambic trimeter—the rhyme scheme is almost nonexistent. There are two imperfect or "near" rhymes (tomb-room; rooms-names) but not one perfect rhyme (see *rhyme*, p. 23). The main aspect of the poem is its cerebration over a fine point, that is, the nature of truth and beauty and the suggestion of the ultimate futility involved in the pursuit of either. Our response to the poem is *both* intellectual and emotional; we feel the emotion of death itself because of the bizarre, grotesque setting of the poem—two people talking to each other in their adjacent tombs. But we are, curiously perhaps, even more stimulated by the poem's message.

To write about poetry we need to probe our initial responses to a poem very carefully. Sometimes we find that we have made some kind of understandable mistake in our first reading. But if we at first feel an overwhelming sadness, and upon rereading and further consideration we *still* feel a great sadness, we should then try to discover the sources of our feelings about the poem. Sometimes a poem has a private meaning for a reader and thus his response is an extremely individualized one. If this is the case, it must be so recognized and stated, then balanced by a more objective description. There is a public and a private response to a poem, the first connected to the poet's obvious intentions and the second influenced by an individual reader's personal experiences.

Analyzing poetry begins with asking questions. What is the poet trying to say? How do we feel when we read the poem? What kind of language does the poet use? Is the poem conventional? Why is the poem so disruptive of my self-complacency? What is it about the poem that excites me? After the student asks as many questions as he can think of, he should formulate some tentative answers. The process is not synthetic or easy, and many questions have no ready answers. With this in mind, let us turn our attention to some of the major poetic techniques.

What Makes a Poem Art?

The answer to the question "What makes a poem art?" is not simple. To begin, we need to know what art is. Broadly defined, art is a *craft* which uses certain *principles and methods* to fashion a particular product which can be evaluated by aesthetic criteria. But precisely how do we account for *poetry* as art? What are the ingredients of poetry which enable us to talk about it as art? There seem to be three categories of knowledge with which we need to familiarize ourselves in order to draw conclusions about poetry as art. Firstly, there are certain established *poetic techniques* or *methods* available to the poet as he carefully fashions his poem. A painter needs to know something about perspective in order to draw a railroad track going off into the distance. Similarly, a poet needs to know something about *ambiguity,* when he attempts to compose a poem with a plurality of possible meanings. Just as we can learn more about the painting of the railroad tracks by following the artist in his learning and trying to learn about perspective, so too we may better understand the art of an ambiguous poem by trying to understand the *device* known as *poetic ambiguity.* Learning some of the poet's methods of artistic creation constitutes our first entrance into the large question of poetry as art.

A second approach is to familiarize ourselves with various specific *genres of poetry*. There are specific kinds of poems which have definite *generic conventions*. When Milton decided to write *an elegy* ("Lycidas"), there were certain things he had to do, or at least which were conventionally done by poets who wrote elegies. A particular kind of poem—an *epic* poem, a *lyric*, a *pastoral* poem, a *sonnet*—has a particular artistic framework with which each poet who takes up the genre must begin. The poet familiarizes himself with all of the special conventions of the genre, and tries to use that genre in his own individual way. Here the *artist* in the poet is realized. By understanding some of the important conventions of different genres, we can begin to move closer to the *materials of poetic composition* and therefore closer to an enlarged understanding of poetry as art.

Thirdly, and finally, we need to consider the exact ways in which a particular poet modifies certain generic conventions, or the ways in which he does new things with the established concepts. Invention is the lifeblood of poetry. What is the poet free to do? What are the limits within which he must work? How does he decide whether to use rhyme? How conventional or regular is his meter? If he chooses to have an irregular meter, what seems to be the *artistic* explanation for his choice?

Though our basic approach, in other words, should be formalistic, we want also to emphasize the internal dynamics created by expressive variation; for example, we need to know about *slant rhyme* as a variation of *exact rhyme, foot substitution* as a deliberate expressive device, about other legitimate meters besides the traditional one, and, finally, about all the various life-giving liberties taken within the established genres and conventions. By understanding, then, the basic poetic techniques, the generic conventions, and the individual modifications of those conventions, we can involve ourselves satisfactorily in *poetry as art*.

Rhyme

Consider the following two poems, the first by Samuel Coleridge (1772–1834) and the second by Walt Whitman (1819–1892).

THE FRUIT PLUCKER

Encinctured with a twine of leaves,
That leafy twine his only dress,
A lovely Boy was plucking fruits,
By moonlight, in a wilderness.

The moon was bright, the air was free,
And fruits and flowers together grew
On many a shrub and many a tree:
And all put on a gentle hue,
Hanging in the shadowy air
Like a picture rich and rare.

It was a climate where, they say,
The night is more beloved than day.

But who that beauteous Boy beguiled,
That beauteous Boy to linger here?
Alone, by night, a little child,
In place so silent and so wild—
Has he no friend, no loving mother near?

AS TOILSOME I WANDER'D VIRGINIA'S WOODS

As toilsome I wander'd Virginia's woods,
To the music of rustling leaves kick'd by my feet, (for 'twas autumn,)
I mark'd at the foot of a tree the grave of a soldier;
Mortally wounded he and buried on the retreat, (easily all could I understand,)
The halt of a mid-day hour, when up! no time to lose—yet this sign left,
On a tablet scrawl'd and nail'd on the tree by the grave,
Bold, cautious, true, and my loving comrade.

Long, long I muse, then on my way go wandering,
Many a changeful season to follow, and many a scene of life,
Yet at times through changeful season and scene, abrupt, alone, or in the crowded street,

Comes before me the unknown soldier's grave, comes the inscription rude in Virginia's woods,
Bold, cautious, true, and my loving comrade.

Thinking back to the "sound identities" of these two poems, how aware were you of the extremely large number of different rhymes introduced in Coleridge's poem? Wasn't your reaction, though perhaps not consciously articulated, "this poem rhymes," without actual consideration of the unusually large *number* of rhymes? And reading Walt Whitman's poem, didn't you find yourself feeling that it *almost* rhymed? Isn't the cadence of Whitman's poem so hypnotizing that you hardly stop to consider whether or not the poem rhymes? When you honestly reflect on your responses to each poem, you probably will begin to realize that, in general, awareness of a poem's rhyme is often imprecise. Many students remember that Whitman's "O Captain, My Captain" rhymed, but do they also remember exactly *how* it rhymed? In other words, we respond to rhyme in a rather private, emotional way, sometimes simply feeling either all sing-songy or half-dead.

When we are *writing* about poetry, we need to be more precise. Rhyme is something we can discuss with a good deal of technical precision.

Rhyme Scheme

Conventionally, we explain the rhyme of a poem by determining its *rhyme scheme,* or pattern of rhyming sounds. We label the sound at the end of the first line with the letter *a* and we continue to assign the letter *a* to the ends of lines in the poem which have the same sound. If the first and third lines of the poem are "green" and "queen," for example, they are both labeled *a.* The second sound we hear at the end of a line is labeled *b,* the next *c,* and so forth. Many poems begin with two rhymes in the first four lines (the possibilities: *abab, aabb, abba*). The rhyme scheme of Coleridge's "The Fruit Plucker" is quite unusual because, for a relatively short poem (seventeen lines), it contains an extremely large number of different rhyming sounds and even two unrhymed ones (lines 1 and 3). Taking the final sound of each line, we assign them letters as follows:

leaves	*a*
dress	*b*
fruits	*c*
ness	*b*
free	*d*
grew	*e*
tree	*d*
hue	*e*
air	*f*
rare	*f*
say	*g*
day	*g*
guiled	*h*
here	*i*
child	*h*
wild	*h*
near	*i*

We summarize the rhyme of the poem by writing that its rhyme scheme is *abcbdedeff gg hihhi*. This is the pattern of the poem's rhyming words. When we apply the same test to Whitman's Civil War poem, we discover that no real rhyme scheme exists, though there is the echoing of "feet," "retreat," and "street" in lines 2, 4, and 10. Repetition and various metrical effects make the poem move swiftly without rhyme. Whitman writes in unusually long lines, giving his poetry an expansiveness sometimes generated through rhyme in poems of shorter lines.

Coleridge's poem, with its multiple rhymes, presents us with an almost magical setting—the sight of a beautiful Boy (note the capitals: this is Boy, period, not just *any boy*) dressed in twines and picking fruits. The scene ("a picture rich and rare") is lush, romantic, inspiring, and beautiful. Rhyme seems to enhance the light and joyous atmosphere of the poem; rhyme makes it a kind of musical celebration. Whitman's sentimental recollection of a dead soldier and his comrade's rude tribute is sombre and pensive; it is meant to be more of a philosophical reflection than a song (this is not to imply that all philosophical poetry does not rhyme while joyous poetry does; we all know that this is not true). The point remains that there is often a relationship between sound and sense. When writing about a poem's rhyme, or lack of rhyme, we should always try to make a case for or against the appropriateness of the poet's decision regarding the use of rhyme. That is, we need to define the rhyme scheme, and then try to *account* for it.

Conventional Rhyme Schemes

There are a few rhyme schemes which have been used again and again in English poetry. Before suggesting, however, that a poem rhymes in a particular way for such-and-such a reason, one should first ask whether it is one of the following *conventional* rhyme schemes.

The most famous of all rhyme schemes is that of the *Shakespearian sonnet.* All sonnets have fourteen lines of iambic pentameter (see *meter,* p. 28). In Shakespeare's sonnets the rhyme scheme is as follows: *abab cdcd efef gg.* This scheme is conventionally divided into *three quatrains* (a quatrain is a stanza of four rhymed or unrhymed lines) and a final *couplet* (two lines, usually rhymed). Thus, the first quatrain rhymes *abab;* the second quatrain, *cdcd,* the third quatrain, *efef,* and the closing couplet, *ee.* Consider, for example, the following well-known sonnet by Shakespeare (1564–1616):

Shall I compare thee to a summer's Day? *a*
Thou art more lovely and more temperate: *b*
Rough winds do shake the darling buds of May, *a*
And summer's lease hath all too short a date: *b*
Sometime too hot the eye of heaven shines, *c*
And often is his gold complexion dimm'd; *d*
And every fair from fair sometimes declines, *e*
By chance or nature's changing course untrimm'd: *d*

But thy eternal summer shall not fade *e*
Nor lose possession of that fair thou ow'st; *f*
Nor shall death brag thou wander'st in his shade, *e*
When in eternal lines to time thou grow'st: *f*
So long as men can breathe, or eyes can see, *g*
So long lives this, and this gives life to thee. *g*

The *Shakespearian sonnet,* also sometimes rather loosely called the *Elizabethan sonnet,* has long been the favorite sonnet form. Before Shakespeare, however, the *Italian* or *Petrarchan sonnet* was popular. Instead of three quatrains and a couplet, the Petrarchan sonnet had an *octave* (or *octet,* eight lines, sometimes a stanza, and sometimes simply the first eight lines of a sonnet) rhyming *abbaabba* and a *sestet* (six lines; the minor division of the Italian sonnet) rhyming in various ways, but most commonly *cdecde.* Another conventional sonnet is the *Spenserian sonnet* in which the rhymes "overlap" each other—*ababbcbccdcdee.* Spenser (1552?–1599) also introduced another famous (and now conventional) rhyme scheme into English poetry when, in *The Fairie Queene,* he invented a stanza (now called the *Spenserian stanza*) consisting of nine iambic lines, the last line being one poetic foot longer than the other eight (the first eight being pentameter, and the ninth being hexameter; see *meter,* p. 27).

There are very few poets who have not tried, at one time or another—and usually in their youth—to write sonnets, and in the majority of cases one of the aforementioned rhyme schemes has been used. Thus while the Petrarchan sonnet was in vogue in the sixteenth century, it is not at all surprising to find it being utilized by the nineteenth-century English poet Gerard Manley Hopkins (1844–1889):

GOD'S GRANDEUR

The world is charged with the grandeur of God. *a*
It will flame out, like shining from shook foil; *b*
It gathers to a greatness, like the ooze of oil *b*
Crushed. Why do men then now not reck his rod? *a*
Generations have trod, have trod, have trod; *a*

And all is seared with trade; bleared, smeared with toil; *b*
And wears man's smudge and shares man's smell: the soil *b*
Is bare now, nor can foot feel, being shod. *a*
And for all this, nature is never spent; *c*
There lives the dearest freshness deep down things; *d*
And though the last lights off the black West went *e*
Oh, morning, at the brown brink eastward, springs— *c*
Because the Holy Ghost over the bent *d*
World broods with warm breast and with ah! bright wings. *e*

As is characteristic of Hopkins, there is a great deal of experimentation taking place in this poem—with words, repetition, sounds, punctuation, etc.—but the main outline is determined by the rhyme scheme of the Petrarchan sonnet.

Another conventional rhyme scheme, which like the Petrarchan sonnet was imported from Italy into England, is *aba, bcb, cdc,* with the second line of a three-line stanza providing the rhyme for the successive stanza. Not very many poets have experimented with this rhyme scheme, invented by Dante, and still known by its Italian name, *terza rima.* The three-line stanzas of *terza rima* are known as *tercets.* Most poets avoid the tercet (it even *sounds* like an odd bird), and instead shorten to couplets or lengthen to quatrains or longer stanzas of differing lengths. Most rhyming quatrains are either of the rhyme scheme *abab* or *abcb* (*a* and *c* being unrhymed lines). In this second kind, we find the *ballad meter,* the *elegiac stanza,* and the *heroic quatrain*—four lines of iambic pentameter rhyming *abab.* There is also the *abba* quatrain in which Tennyson's *In Memoriam* is written.

A conventional rhyme scheme, which once enjoyed great popularity and which has been used imaginatively by many of the best English poets, is *rhyme royal.* This stanza, sometimes called the *Chaucerian stanza* or the *Troilus stanza* (because of its use in Chaucer's *Troilus and Cressida*), and seldom encountered in modern poetry, consists of seven iambic pentameter lines (see *meter,* p. 25), rhyming *ababbcc.* A good example is found in the opening stanza of a ballad by Chaucer (1340–1400) in which the poet-singer advises certain women to hide their beauties because Alceste is here and her bright beauty puts all others to shame:

Hyde, Absolon, thy gilte tresses clere; *a*
Ester, let thou thy meknesse al a-doun; *b*
Hyd, Jonathas, al thy frendly manere; *a*
Penalopee, and Marcia Catoun, *b*
Mak of your wyfhood no comparisoun; *b*
Hyde ye your beauties, Isoude and Eleyne, *c*
Alceste is here, that al that may desteyne. *c*

Finally, numerous poets have attempted to write poems in an eight iambic line stanza rhyming *abababcc,* which is known as *ottava rima.* This stanza was used extensively by the Italian poet Boccaccio (1313–1375) in his *Teseida* (1340–1342) and his *Filostrato* (1339–1340).

All of these conventional rhyme schemes appear, disappear, and then reappear during the passage of poetry through time. (Also see *free verse* in the next section.)

Further Terms for Discussing Rhyme

We now know how to determine a rhyme scheme, and we have looked at some of the conventional ones. In addition, we need to know that the rhymes themselves can be differentiated from one another with further terms from the vocabulary of literary analysis.

SINGLE, DOUBLE, AND TRIPLE RHYME. When the last pronounced syllable of one line rhymes with the last pronounced syllable of another line, it is known as *single rhyme.* For example, "green" with "queen." *Double rhyme* occurs when the last two pronounced syllables of one line *both* rhyme with the last two pronounced syllables of another line. Sometimes these rhymes are termed *disyllabic.* Thus, "benighted" with "delighted," "master" with "disaster," or "airy" with "fairy." *Triple rhyme* (*trisyllabic*), as by now you have probably guessed, refers to the rhyming of the last three pronounced syllables of one line with the last three pronounced sÿllables of another line—"Sir Pleasure" with "her measure," for instance. Instances of trisyllabic rhyme are relatively rare (as my example perhaps suggests).

END-STOPPING AND ENJAMBEMENT. When a line and a sentence end together, the line is said to be *end-stopped.* When a sentence advances into the next line, it is an instance of *enjambement.* For example, in the following couplet from *The Rape of the Lock* by Alexander Pope (1688–1744) the first line is enjambed, the second line, end-stopped:

> For spirits, freed from mortal laws, with ease
> Assume what sexes and what shapes they please.

In "The Haystack in the Floods" by William Morris (1834–1896), we find an end-stopped couplet and then enjambement as the second line of the second couplet continues into the third:

> Had she come all the way for this,
> To part at last without a kiss?
> Yea, had she borne the dirt and rain
> That her own eyes might see him slain
> Beside the haystack in the floods?

Rhyme has as much bearing on meaning as it does on organization, and thus considerations of end-stopping should attempt to determine why the poet chooses to have his thought end with his rhyme; rhyme works both as a device for organizing words and as an instrument for sharpening the sense of an idea. End-stopping and enjambement have as much, if not more, to do with rhythm as with rhyme. Students should try to detect, therefore, the rhythmical effects which the poet is trying to achieve.

MASCULINE AND FEMININE RHYME. When there is stress (emphasis) on the last syllable of the rhyme, it is *masculine;* when there is no stress, it is *feminine.* A *stressed syllable* followed by an *unstressed syllable,* in other words, produces feminine rhyme. Often a poet mixes feminine rhyme with masculine rhyme. Consider, for example, the resulting mixture in the following stanza from "Soliloquy of the Spanish Cloister" by Robert Browning (1812–1889); in the odd-numbered lines, the emphasis (stress) is placed on the next-to-last syllable—producing feminine rhymes

—and in the even-numbered lines the emphasis is placed on the last syllable—producing masculine rhymes:

There's a great text in Galatians,	(*feminine*)
Once you trip on it, entails	(*masculine*)
Twenty-nine distinct damnations,	(*feminine*)
One sure, if another fails;	(*masculine*)
If I trip him just a-dying,	(*feminine*)
Sure of heaven as sure can be,	(*masculine*)
Spin him round and send him flying	(*feminine*)
Off to hell, a Manichee?	(*masculine*)

INTERNAL AND TERMINAL RHYME. As distinguished from the majority of rhymes—those which end lines and are known as *terminal rhymes*—we also have *internal rhymes*, that is, sounds within a line which rhyme with one another or with the sound at the end of the line, as for example, in the third line of this stanza from Coleridge's "The Rime of the Ancient Mariner":

> The harbour-bay was clear as glass,
> So smoothly was it strewn!
> And on the bay the moonlight lay   (*bay, lay*—internal rhyme)
> And the shadow of the moon.

Or again, from the same poem, notice the use of internal rhyme in lines three and five:

> And I had done a hellish thing,
> And it would work 'em woe:
> For all averred, I had killed the bird   (*averred, bird*)
> That made the breeze to blow.
> Ah wretch! said they, the bird to slay,   (*they, slay*)
> That made the breeze to blow!

PERFECT AND IMPERFECT (SLANT) RHYME. When the sound of one word is *exactly* the same as the sound of the word with which it is meant to rhyme, it is known as *perfect rhyme*—as, for example, in the rhyming of "they" with "slay" in the lines above. When a sound is not quite the same as the rhyming sound, it is known as *slanted, near,* or *imperfect rhyme,* as, for example, rhyming "long" with "sung." *Slant rhyme* has contributed a great deal to the lifeblood of poetry in the twentieth century.

EUPHONY AND CACOPHONY. While rhyme is our major concern when considering the sounds which a poem makes, there are other related kinds of sound. *Euphony* is the quality produced by soft, smooth, pleasing sounds which "fit" well together, as, for example, in the opening lines of "London Snow" by Robert Bridges (1844–1930):

> While men were all asleep the snow came flying,
> In large white flakes falling on the city brown,
> Stealthily and perpetually settling and loosely lying,
>   Hushing the latest traffic of the drowsy town;
> Deadening, muffling, stifling its murmurs failing;
> Lazily and incessantly floating down and down:
>   Silently sifting and veiling road, roof, and railing;
> Hiding difference, making unevenness even,
> Into angles and crevices softly drifting and sailing.

The sounds are easy to pronounce together. They blend with and support one another. In general, vowel sounds are more apt to generate euphony than consonant sounds. Some "liquid" consonant sounds also produce smoothness—such as the vowels *l, m, n, r, y,* and *w.* Notice also in Bridges' lines the use of *alliteration,* the repetition of two or more of the same sounds within a line ("*l*oosely *l*ying," "*r*oad, *r*oof, and *r*ailing"). Alliteration is frequently used to create a liquidity, a euphonious sound. One should realize that meter can also aid in achieving euphony. It is logical that a line which *scans* regularly (see *meter,* p. 25), that is, which divides the line—and thus its sounds—in an orderly way, is more euphonious than an irregular or rough line. We might also observe that some of the euphony in Bridges' poem is created by the *imagined sound of the flying snow.*

The opposite of euphony is *cacophony,* the quality produced by the use of dissimilar, harsh, disruptive, or dissonant sounds which do *not* blend with each other. John Donne (1572–1631) uses cacophony in the opening lines of "The Canonization"; here we discover a set of sounds which, in their rude conjunction, makes us sit up at attention:

> For Godsake hold your tongue and let me love,
>   Or chide my palsy or my gout,
> My five gray hairs or ruin'd fortune flout,
>   With wealth your state, your mind with Arts improve,
>   Take you a course, get you a place . . .

BLANK VERSE. There are some forms of poetry which do without rhyme entirely, and no other kind of poetry has been so widely attempted as that written in *blank verse,* unrhymed lines of iambic pentameter (see *meter,* below). It is perhaps somewhat ironic that so much of the best of English literature—from the plays of Christopher Marlow to Milton's *Paradise Lost* and Wordsworth's *The Prelude*—has been written in poetry which does not rhyme. A further discussion of blank verse appears in the next section.

Meter

There are traditional patterns of stress in poetry, and meter has to do with the basic, regular rhythms of poetry. The alternation of stressed and unstressed syllables within a line of poetry follows certain established forms. A unit of stressed and unstressed syllables, that is, a unit which is identifiable and repeated, is known as a *poetic foot.* We should also keep in mind that while there are *basic metrical patterns,* there is also a great deal of *expressive rhythmic variation* which often makes poetry invigorating and unpredictable. We determine the *number of poetic feet* a line of poetry contains by counting the syllabic units which are repeated in the line. *Stressed syllables* are indicated by the acute accent mark ′, and *unstressed syllables* by ˘. We use these two marks as the main symbols of an established system of describing rhythm in poetry. This system, called *scansion,* uses the visual symbols ′ and ˘ to indicate stressed and unstressed syllables. A third symbol is || and represents the *caesura,* or the metrical "break" (pause) in a line of poetry (not all lines have a caesura, and it is not really customary to cite it when it does appear). The names of the kinds of poetic feet are as follows:

Iambic. Iambic is the most commonly used metrical unit of poetry written in the English language and refers to a unit of two syllables, the first unstressed and the second stressed:

> dĕfý *one iambic foot* (an *iamb*)

We *scan* the lines of poetry by indicating the stressed and unstressed syllables and then marking them off as poetic feet:

> Whăt béck'/nĭng ghóst,/ălóng/thĕ móon-/lĭght sháde
> Ĭnvítes/my̆ stéps,/ănd póints/tŏ yón/dĕr gláde?
> (Alexander Pope)

Trochaic. Trochaic refers to a unit of two syllables, the first stressed and the second unstressed (that is, the opposite of iambic):

> dwéllĭng *one trochaic foot* (a *trochee*)
> Spín hĭm/róund ănd/sénd hĭm/flýĭng

Spondaic. Spondaic refers to a unit of two syllables, *both* of which are stressed. It is rarely used throughout an entire line of poetry (with *no* unstressed syllables, a line would be almost impossible to read). Instead it is placed in a line mainly written in a different meter. Often it is used as the first foot of a line in another meter and when one foot, a *spondee,* for example, is used in place of the regular foot—an *iamb,* for example—we say that the poet has *substituted* a spondaic for an iambic foot. We speak, then, of *metrical substitutions.* In the following line, a spondee has been substituted for the first iambic foot:

> Héighó,/thĕ tále/wăs áll/ă líe.
> (A. E. Housman)

Trochaic substitutions are also very common. While there are three kinds of poetic feet consisting of two syllables (iambic, trochaic, spondaic), there are only two kinds of feet consisting of three syllables, the *dactylic* and the *anapestic*.

DACTYLIC. Dactylic refers to a unit of three syllables, consisting of one stressed syllable followed by two unstressed syllables:

cárefŭllў *one dactylic foot* (a *dactyl*)

ANAPESTIC. Anapestic refers to a unit of three syllables, consisting of two unstressed syllables followed by one stressed syllable:

tŏ thĕ shóre *one anapestic foot* (an *anapest*)

Often an anapest is mixed with iambic, particularly in the beginning of "ballad" type lines. For example, notice how an anapest is used to lead into each of the following lines of iambic:

Thĕre ăre thíngs/ŏf whích/Ĭ máy/nŏt spéak;
Thĕre ăre dréams/thăt cán/nŏt díe;
Thĕre ăre thóughts/thăt máke/thĕ stróng/hĕarts wéak
(Longfellow)

Counting Poetic Feet

In addition to scanning the lines of a poem and dividing them into feet, we need to acknowledge the number of feet in a line by using the following terms:

monometer—one foot in a line
dimeter—two feet in a line
trimeter—three feet in a line
tetrameter—four feet in a line
pentameter—five feet in a line
hexameter—six feet in a line
heptameter—seven feet in a line
octameter—eight feet in a line

Consider the following two lines:

> W̆ith hów/săd stéps,/Ŏ Móon,/thŏu clímb'st/thĕ skíes,
> Hŏw sí/lĕntlý,/ănd wíth/hŏw wán/ă fáce.
>
> (Sir Philip Sidney, 1554–1586)

Each line has five feet, and thus the lines are written in *pentameter*. Because the meter is *iambic*, we may describe the lines in full by designating them as *iambic pentameter*. A few other examples follow; the first line has been scanned; for practice, try to scan the others:

IAMBIC PENTAMETER.

> Thĕ cúr/fĕw tólls/thĕ knéll/ŏf párt/ĭng dáy,
> The lowing herd wind slowly o'er the lea,
> The plowman homeward plods his weary way,
> And leaves the world to darkness and to me.
>
> (Thomas Gray, 1716–1771)

BLANK VERSE (*Unrhyming Iambic Pentameter*).

> Sŏmethíng/thĕre ís/thăt dóes/n'̆t lóve/ă wáll,*
> That sends the frozen-ground-swell under it,
> And spills the upper boulders in the sun;
> And makes gaps even two can pass abreast.
>
> (Robert Frost, 1874–1963)

IAMBIC TETRAMETER.

> Evĕn súch/ĭs tíme,/thăt tákes/ĭn trúst
> Our youth, our joys, our all we have,
> And pays us but with age and dust;
> Who, in the dark and silent grave,
> When we have wandered all our ways,

* The first word could also be read as a spondee: Sómethíng.

Shuts up the story of our days.
But from this earth, this grave, this dust,
My God shall raise me up, I trust.
(John Lyly, 1554?–1606)

VARIATION OF LINE LENGTH (*Iambic*).

	number of feet
Hárk, hárk!/thĕ lárk/ăt héaven's/găte síngs.	4
And Phoebus gins arise,	3
His steeds to water at those springs	4
On chaliced flowers that lies;	3
And winking May-buds begin	4
To ope their golden eyes:	3
When everything that pretty is,	4
My lady, sweet, arise!	3
Arise, arise!	2

(Shakespeare)

TROCHAIC TRIMETER WITH A VARIATION. In the following lines by William Blake (1757–1827), we find, beginning with the third line, a change in the third foot; if we place no stress on the last syllable, we find that the third foot is a *dactyl* being substituted for a *trochee;* if we place stress on the last syllable, we have an irregularity. Try to read the poem aloud and then scan it; the basic unit is trochaic:

Little lamb, who made thee?
Dost thou know who made thee,
Gave thee life, and bid thee feed
By the stream and o'er the mead;
Gave thee clothing of delight,
Softest clothing, wooly, bright;
Gave thee such a tender voice,
Making all the vales rejoice?
Little lamb, who made thee?
Dost thou know who made thee?

COMBINING IAMBIC PENTAMETER WITH IAMBIC TRIMETER.

The stormy evening closes now in vain,
Loud wails the wind and beats the driving rain,
While here in sheltered house
With fire ypainted walls,
I hear the wind abroad,
I hark the calling squalls—
"Blow, blow," I cry, "you burst your cheeks in vain!"
"Blow, blow," I cry, "my love is home again!"
(Robert Louis Stevenson, 1850–1894)

These, then, are some examples. For practice, try scanning a poem whenever you come upon it. Remember, too, that scansion is imperfect because poetry itself is sometimes imperfect in its rhythms. A poet often needs a word that does not quite fit; he prefers having irregularity of meter to forfeiting the word. Poets often break from their meter and then return to it. A reader should not try to force meter onto a line of poetry. Sometimes the line simply does not want to be scanned in a particular way, but instead is a combination of stresses randomly placed. Try always to read a line of poetry honestly and sensibly, then see whether it falls into a basic pattern.

Poetic Techniques

When a poet has decided on rhyme scheme and meter, he needs to begin making other artistic decisions, namely, which, if any, of various other poetic techniques he should employ. Some of these follow:

ALLITERATION. As we have already noted, this is the repetition of similar sounds or syllables near to each other in a poem (in a line or line group). The opening of Shakespeare's well-known song from *The Tempest* is a good example: "*F*ull *f*athom *f*ive thy *f*ather lies." The most conventional kind of alliteration is that in which the like sounds are at the beginning of the words; the repetition of initial sounds is called *initial rhyme* (as with Shakespeare's "f"s).

ALLUSION. This is the method of tacitly referring to particular people, places, works of literature, familiar objects, and so on. The technique is used for various reasons—sometimes to show a kind of erudition, sometimes to achieve an expansiveness in the poetic world being created (the main use of the heavy allusion in Milton's *Paradise Lost*). There are distinctions to bear in mind: purely "literary" allusions (as in Eliot's *The Wasteland*), simple references (as to the trinitarian doctrine of Donne), satiric concealment (as we shall notice in Auden), and symbolic allusions (the "two-handed engine" in Milton's "Lycidas").

In general, allusions tend to magnify a poetic world, transform it into something larger and more inclusive. An allusion can be obvious or it can be *hidden.* While busily interpreting the meaning behind those allusions about which they agree, many readers of T. S. Eliot's poetry are still combing his lines for hidden literary allusions.

An allusion does not need to be specifically presented. While a poet might, for example, allude to *Psalms* directly (a definite Biblical allusion), he might also simply refer to something in a prosaic, less precise way—as when John Donne opens one of his "Holy Sonnets" in this way: "Batter my heart, three-person'd God." Here Donne is referring (alluding) to the trinitarian ("three-person'd") concept of God as Father, Son, and Holy Ghost. An allusion usually adds to the strength of an image; consider the use of the following allusion as Milton (1608–1674) describes the meeting of Satan and Death in *Paradise Lost:*

> . . . and such a frown
> Each cast at th'other, as when two black clouds
> With Heav'n's Artillery fraught, came rattling on
> Over the *Caspian* . . .

Here Milton has *alluded,* by way of a Homeric (epic) simile, to the Caspian Sea which his erudite readers would long have associated with terrible, dark storminess (as early as a reference in Horace, *Odes,* II, 9.12). The allusion serves to make the clashing of Satan and Death dramatically visual. The clash is dynamically magnified through the allusion.

Sometimes an allusion is masked or imprecise, though the exact reference is generally well understood. This is particularly true in satirical verse when the poet wishes to attack something (or someone) specifically, but does not want to be accused of doing so; thus he makes his allusions obscure (or veiled). When W. H. Auden (1907–) satirized the death-by-boredom of a common individual in America, his famous "unknown citizen," he says of him: "He worked in a factory and never got fired,/ But satisfied his employers, Fudge Motors, Inc." We can all guess what company Auden was really alluding to.

Allusion, then, is a complex but all-important device in poetic composition. The poet can use allusions to strengthen images, to broaden the world of the poem, to define the characters and setting, or even simply to make his poem more "learned" and challenging to well-educated readers. Some allusions in poetry are never completely understood. There have been over fifty scholarly articles, for example, trying to explain a single allusion to the two-handed engine in Milton's "Lycidas."

AMBIGUITY. This is the device of trying to suggest more than one meaning (multiple meanings). That is, a poet intentionally suggests alternative meanings for a term or perhaps for an entire poem. Ambiguity, introduced as a critical term by William Empson, has become one of the modern poet's favorite devices, perhaps because it allows the poet to determine just how much of what he is thinking he wishes to share completely with the reader. To suggest many meanings with one word is of course fun, and the readers of a poem need to inquire which, if any, of the meanings was intended to dominate. Through the discussion of a poem's possible meanings, one usually arrives at an enlarged understanding of it.

Intentional ambiguity, the deliberate creation of different or competing meanings, is a device which the poet can easily adopt. "Punning" is one common type of verbal ambiguity. *Accidental ambiguity,* on the other hand, is simply a failure of the poet to communicate his meaning carefully. It is usually apparent from the general structure and movement of a poem whether accidental ambiguity is involved; nine times out of ten, ambiguity *is* intentional. Consider, for example, Robert Frost's little poem,

FIRE AND ICE

Some say the world will end in fire,
Some say in ice.
From what I've tasted of desire
I hold with those who favor fire.
But if I had to perish twice,
I think I know enough of hate
To say that for destruction ice
Is also great
And would suffice.

One of the reasons this poem is exciting is that it is intentionally ambiguous. In the first place, it is not totally clear whether the speaker would prefer fire or ice in the end; what does it *mean* to think of the world perishing twice? How is that possible? Further, just what *is* fire, and what *is* ice (in this poem)? The metaphors have an *intentional* ambiguity. First it seems that fire is meant to be associated with burning, passionate love or desire, but then it seems that fire also suggests a kind of burning hatred. The poem acquires further ambiguity through the conventional connotations of the words "fire" and "ice" (a connotation is a secondary, implied, or associated meaning). By using ambiguity Frost has written an exciting, challenging poem. Every interpretation will be new and different, for Frost has purposely left much room for creative guesswork.

ANTITHESIS. When a poet deliberately joins opposites, or associates things which are not ordinarily associated, antithesis results. The poet deliberately joins together opposites in order to create tension, or, simply because, as Aristotle and others have advised, contrasts are easily understood. Many aesthetic philosophers believe that all art requires tension of some kind, and poetry is no exception. This is not to imply that all poetry uses antithesis, for, in fact, much of it does not. Antithesis was popular in English poetry in the eighteenth century and has some followers today, but the student will not encounter it too many times. The problem with antithesis is that in order to gain tension (and sometimes even attention), the poet risks sacrificing subtlety. This does not have to be true. In Frost's short poem, fire and ice are held in exciting opposition. The competition between them generates a stimulating tension in the poem. In its earlier uses, however, antithesis often strikes the modern reader as appropriate, but also, unfortunately, wooden. Consider, for example, the following lines by Pope, one of the English poets most responsible for the massive experimentation with antithesis; this is a description of Man, with a capital "M":

> In doubt to deem himself a God, or Beast;
> In doubt his Mind or Body to prefer;
> Born but to die, and reas'ning but to err;
> Alike in ignorance, his reason such,
> Whether he thinks too little, or too much
> Sole judge of Truth, in endless Error hurl'd:
> The glory, jest, and riddle of the world!

By joining together series of opposites—God—Beast; Mind—Body; ignorance—reason—Pope aptly summarizes the multiple contradictions inevitably arising out of man the animal and human being.

ARCHETYPES. An archetype is, literally, the arch or main type of the others in that the others copy, borrow, and preserve the essential characteristics of the original. Images that recur throughout all literature become symbols. Light is a symbol of goodness, while dark is a symbol of evil. A river means certain things to everyone; winding its way along, it traditionally is used to symbolize the concept or idea of the *ceaseless journey*, the mood of *timelessness*. The Phoenix, a mythological bird said to be reborn from its own ashes, generally represents the idea of rebirth. Basic images, like the river or the Phoenix, when well enough known and used in poetry, become stabilized as symbols or images with universal characteristics and connotations. Certain scenes and situations, using those symbols, become *archetypal* to the extent that they are associated with the symbolic action or activity of that scene—for example, the Garden of Eden is the archetype for creation, for life and nature before the Fall, and other settings trying to suggest creation borrow characteristics from the Garden of Eden. As archetype in poetry may take any form. It may be an action (for example, rebirth), a setting (Eden), a character (the devil), or an object (arrow), and it must have universal meaning (theories of archetypal interpretation of literature were skillfully developed by Maud Bodkin who applied certain psychological precepts to literary criticism).

CACOPHONY (see discussion under *rhyme*, p. 24).

CONCEIT. This is one of the more slippery terms to invade the language of literary analysis. Originating from "concept," a conceit is now thought of as a particular kind of image, a picture of one thing used to suggest another, the real thing, or to evoke a particular atmosphere. When one *images* (makes an image of) something, one usually employs figurative language. This is a symbolic process. When discussing an image, we may comment on its nature, the representation it is intended to have, and on its appropriateness in light of the theme.

Our judgment of appropriateness often requires investigation into the connotations of the terms of the image during the period of time when the poem was written. The late Rosamund Tuve made an enormous contribution to literary criticism by analyzing the probable contemporary understanding of certain images of seventeenth-century poetry.

A conceit, a particularly difficult or challenging image, usually presents a bizarre picture of reality or a widely imaginative comparison. *Petrarchan conceits* were unusual ways of expressing *love*, and were very popular with the Elizabethan sonneteers. The term "metaphysical," first introduced into literary criticism by John Dryden (1631–1700), was applied to "conceit" by Dr. Samuel Johnson (1709–1784) in his eighteenth-century *Life of Cowley*. A *metaphysical conceit*, the kind which now receives the greatest amount of attention from literary critics, was explained by Johnson as the yoking together of disparate objects, that is, a comparison between things *rarely considered in conjunction*. The most famous metaphysical conceit is that of the twin compasses in John Donne's "A Valediction: Forbidding Mourning." In this poem, a lover imaginatively pictures his soul as one end of a mathematician's compass running around in a circle formed around the other fixed point of the compass that represents his beloved's soul. The conceit is extraordinarily unusual and unconventional; this simply is not a natural or customary way of talking about love:

> Our two souls therefore, which are one,
> Though I must go, endure not yet
> A break, but an expansion,
> Like gold to airy thinness beat.
>
> If they be two, they are two so
> As two stiff compasses are two,
> Thy soul the fixt foot, makes no show
> To move, but doth, if th'other do.
>
> And though in the center sit,
> Yet when the other far doth roam,
> It leans and hearkens after it,
> And grows erect as that comes home.
>
> Such wilt thou be to me who must,
> Like th'other foot, obliquely run;
> Thy firmness makes my circle just,
> And makes me end where I begun.

This metaphysical conceit has become the one against which all others may ultimately be judged in terms of originality and complexity. A modern poet will occasionally use a conceit in order to make his point in an obscure, yet fascinating, way. Sometimes an attack of "obscurantism" will be leveled at the poet who overindulges his wit in the creation of superficially clever conceits. A conceit, to summarize, is an intellectualization of an idea or emotion, an unusually bizarre and dramatic picturing of some relationship.

Euphony (see discussion under *rhyme*, p. 24).

Figurative Language. Figurative language is the opposite of literal language. When a poet is writing figuratively, he says one thing to mean another, or creates certain pictures to enable us to see things more clearly. Recall the opening two lines of the poem we looked at earlier by Lord Byron: "She walks in beauty, like the night/Of cloudless climes and starry skies." The person being described does not *literally* look like the clear, starry night. The poet uses these words, this expression, to help us picture something in a dramatic (and, in this instance, abstract) way. The words enhance the intensity of the lady's beauty. In other words, Byron uses figurative language to suggest qualities which when literally described would not have as much impact.

In general, there are two basic kinds of "figures" which the poet can use, the *simile* and the *metaphor.*

1. Simile. A simile is a comparison—between one thing, person, place, idea, etc., and another—which is introduced by the word "like" or "as." Byron's opening lines constitute a simile because the word "like" is used. In writing about the picture which Byron is painting, we must, then, be sure to refer to it as a simile. We can write about it as "the simile equating his beloved to a cloudless, starry night," or as "the simile in which Byron compares his beloved to a beautiful, cloudless, starry night." We might also recall the simile we cited earlier from Milton's *Paradise Lost:*

> . . . and such a frown
> Each cast at th'other, as when two black Clouds
> With Heav'n's Artillery fraught, came rattling on
> Over the *Caspian* . . .

Here the word *as* signals that Milton is using a simile. We may refer to the lines as "the simile in which Milton compares the meeting of Satan and Death to two clouds clashing over the traditionally stormy Caspian Sea."

A few other examples follow; the words "like" or "as," which directly announce a figurative comparison, in each instance have been italicized:

> Let us go then, you and I,
> When the evening is spread out against the sky
> *Like* a patient etherised upon a table.
>
> (T. S. Eliot)

> The Mind is an enchanting thing
> is an enchanted thing

like the glaze on a
katydid-wing
subdivided by sun
till the nettings are legion.
(Marianne Moore, 1887–)

There's a certain slant of light,
On winter afternoons,
That oppresses, *like* the weight
Of cathedral tunes.
(Emily Dickinson)

Like snowballs tossed,
Like soft white butterflies,
The peonies poise in the twilight.
(John Gould Fletcher, 1886–1950)

As in the midst of battle there is room
For thoughts of love, and in foul sin for mirth,
As gossips whisper of a trinket's worth
Spied by the death-bed's flickering candle-gloom;
As in the crevices of Caesar's tomb
The sweet herbs flourish on a little earth:
So in this great disaster of our birth
We can be happy and forget our doom.
(George Santayana, 1863–1952)

In each instance we discover a simile which is exciting, stimulating, and provocative, and which effectively dramatizes the poet's thoughts. All of the comparisons are apt, creative, and artistic.

2. Metaphor. Unlike a simile, a metaphor does *not* use the words "like" or "as" to make a direct comparison. Instead, the poet usually uses some form of the verb "to be." That is, instead of saying that A is *like* B, the poet simply says, directly or by implication, that A *is* B. To transform Byron's simile into a metaphor, we would simply write that she *is* a beautiful night. The metaphor is like the simile because it establishes a comparison. Sometimes the "is" of a metaphor is implied, and the poet simply talks about A as if it *were* B. In the following ex-

ample, the Victorian poetess Christina Rossetti (1830–1894) pictures floating lilies as little boats for bees; because her comparison is not based on the use of the words "like" or "as," the picture is a metaphorical one. Here is the metaphor:

> There are rivers lapsing down
>   Lily-laden to the sea:
> Every lily *is* a boat
>   For bees, one two, or three.

We write about this picture as "the metaphor in which Christina Rossetti pictures lilies as bees' boats," or "the metaphorical depiction of lilies as bees' boats," etc. A few other examples of metaphor follow:

> Death, what hast thou to do with one for whom
> Time *is* not lord, but servant?
>
> (Algernon Charles Swinburne, 1837–1909)

> I should have *been* a pair of ragged claws
> Scuttling across the floors of silent seas.
>
> (T. S. Eliot)

> This turf is not like turf:
> It *is* a smooth dry carpet of velvet,
> Embroidered with brown patterns of needles and cones.
> These trees are not like trees:
> They *are* innumerable feathery pagoda-umbrellas,
> Stiffly ungracious to the wind,
> Teetering on red-lacquered stems.
>
> (John Gould Fletcher)

Notice how Fletcher here has avoided relying on a simile—this is not *like* what it seems—and instead plunges into metaphor: it *is*; they *are*.

Sometimes a poet skillfully mingles or alternates metaphor and simile. Consider the following lines by George Meredith (1828–1909). He is describing a singing lark, and he begins with a metaphor (a "to be" verb implied in the phrase "the silver chain of sound"), then switches to a simile ("*like* water-dimples").

> He rises and begins to round,
> He drops the silver chain of sound,
> Of many links without a break,
> In chirrup, whistle, slur and shake,
> All intervolved and spreading wide,
> Like water-dimples down a tide
> Where ripple ripple overcurls
> And eddy into eddy whirls.

The sounds of the singing lark are compared to an unbroken chain of sound, but the word "like" itself is not used, and thus the comparison is a metaphor. The sounds, in their linked connection, spread out *like* concentric circles of ripples and eddies in a stream.

3. Hyperbole. In addition to metaphor and simile, a poet may also use a few other devices of figurative speech, one of which is hyperbole, a form of poetic exaggeration. The poet deliberately magnifies something, usually in order to make it dramatic. In the following lines from *Song of Myself*, Walt Whitman uses hyperbole effectively in order to dramatize his self-image. The sun would kill him except that he is also sending out his own bright rays; with a brief twirl of his tongue, he can encompass whole worlds. The exaggeration is striking:

> Dazzling and tremendous how quick the sun-rise would kill me,
> If I could not now and always send sun-rise out of me.
>
> We also ascend dazzling and tremendous as the sun,
> We found our own O my soul in the calm and cool of the daybreak.
>
> My voice goes after what my eyes cannot reach,
> With the twirl of my tongue I encompass worlds and volumes of worlds.

Andrew Marvell (1621–1678) uses hyperbole in "To His Coy Mistress" and thereby suggests dramatically how long it would take to describe his beloved's great beauties:

My vegetable love should grow
Vaster than empires, and more slow;
An hundred years should go to praise
Thine eyes and on thy forehead gaze;
Two hundred to adore each breast,
But thirty thousand to the rest;
An age at least to every part,
And the last she should show your heart.

Hyperbole can be used for almost any purpose, making events more tragic, love greater, funny things funnier, and so forth. Often a simile or a metaphor becomes hyperbolic, because the comparison made or implied constitutes such tremendous exaggeration.

4. Synecdoche. This is a particular kind of metaphor in which a part is used to represent the whole. A salient characteristic or feature of the object is named, but not the object itself (for example, "hooves" instead of horses).

5. Oxymoron. Another figure of speech is known as *oxymoron*, the combining of words or elements with apparently opposite or contradictory meanings. Sometimes a poet will refer to "dark sunlight," or "hating love"; Milton's "darkness visible" and Shakespeare's "O heavy lightness" are good examples. Through oxymoron a poet is able to call attention to the paradoxical nature of certain feelings, concepts, or situations. *Oxymoronic* language has been used extensively by Petrarchan love poets like Henry Howard, Earl of Surrey (1517?–1547), who constantly complained of following a woman he loved, but who nevertheless caused him great unhappiness. Oxymoron is often used to suggest dramatically the quality of love's bittersweetness.

FORESHADOWING. This is the technique of suggesting *early* in a poem (as well as in plays and prose fiction) what will happen *later*. That is, the poet suggests ahead of time what will take place later. A poet often likes to drop hints, and when we write a critical summary of what happens in a poem, we are apt to discuss how the poet "prepares" us for such-and-such. We cite the evidence appearing early in the poem which indicates that the poet knew clearly how he was going to end his poem.

IMAGE. An image has been defined as a mental picture of a sensation. In literature, this mental picture is created by words. C. Day Lewis has simply explained that an image is "a picture made out of words." An image, through repeated use in the same way (sense) becomes a *symbol.* That is, one thing is allowed to stand for (symbolize) another. Images are part of meaning. They define atmosphere, and they support the theme. Usually images participate in a larger *pattern of imagery.* We talk about the *imagery of darkness and light,* for example, in a particular poem (also plays, fiction), and we cite *individual images*—references to light or darkness in some form, from bright emanating rays of sunshine to tiny shadows in corners. Images, then, are figurative depictions or representations of things. Conceits, as we have already explained, are complicated, or intellectualized images. In their simplest definition, images are literally what they suggest—pictures or representations. Plato (427–347 B.C.) describes, in *The Republic,* a scene in which men watch shadows flickering on the wall of a cave. The men are seeing only images of reality, or substitutes for real things. In a poem we find dramatic substitutions for real things. A poet uses images to create an atmosphere in accord with the particular meaning of what is happening in the poem.

For example, in the opening stanza of "Mariana" by Tennyson (1809–1892), Mariana's dreariness is dramatized by images of decay, decline, and loneliness. She is waiting, futilely, for her lover. Images are used to support her emotional condition; that is, instead of discussing her condition literally, Tennyson suggests it through images:

> With blackest moss the flower-pots
>   Were thickly crusted, one and all:
> The rusted nails fell from the knots
>   That held the pear to the gable-wall.
> The broken sheds look'd sad and strange:
>   Unlifted was the clinking latch;
>   Weeded and worn the ancient thatch
> Upon the lonely moated grange.
>   She only said, "My life is dreary,

He cometh not," she said;
She said, "I am aweary, aweary,
I would that I were dead!"

The pictures made out of words here are various images: the image of flower-pots encrusted with black moss, the image of rusty nails, the images of the broken sheds and the untouched latch, and the image of the worn thatch together form a *pattern of imagery* of desolation and neglect. Each image is reinforced by every other image. Each is stronger (more dramatic, more meaningful) in conjunction with the others than it is by itself. Each detail of the description represents something larger, suggests more than is actually stated, and that is the main use of images: they enable us to form mental pictures of emotional situations. Reference to the moss-encrusted flower-pots suggests to us the enormous negligence in Mariana's cottage and generates vividly the atmosphere of unhappiness arising from neglect.

Images advance a basic conception of the poet's mind. For example, in the following line from his poem "Irradiations," John Gould Fletcher uses images to depict the midsummer sky as a kind of ballet or fast, dancing movement:

The iridescent vibrations of midsummer light
Dancing, dancing, suddenly flickering and quivering
Like little feet or the movement of quick hands clapping,
Or the rustle of furbelows or the clash of polished gems.
The palpitant mosaic of the midday light
Colliding, sliding, leaping and lingering:
Oh, I could lie on my back all day,
And mark the mad ballet of the midsummer sky.

The image of light beams darting *like* little feet (notice that Fletcher uses a simile) seems to suggest further images to him, and we witness a series of images almost transforming one another—the movement first figuratively represented as similar to dancing feet is suggested by "quick hands clapping," then by the rustle of furbelows (trimming on a woman's gown) and then, more abstractly, by "the clash of polished gems." Then Fletcher begins again, introducing a second image—a large mosaic of light—to work up to his final conceptualization of the midsummer sky as a "mad ballet." The images all contribute to *the pattern of dance imagery.*

We write, then, about particular images, about the patterns of imagery they form, and about *recurrent patterns of imagery* when certain of the patterns are repeated later in the work in question. Often one or two images sufficiently (or convincingly) create an appropriate atmosphere. In a short poem entitled "The Lonely Death," a minor American poetess, Adelaide Crapsey, deftly uses coldness and unnatural light to picture dramatically the moment of her death:

> In the cold I will rise, I will bathe
> In waters of ice; myself
> Will shiver, and shrive myself,
> Alone in the dawn, and anoint
> Forehead and feet and hands;
> I will shutter the windows from light,
> I will place in their sockets the four
> Tall candles and set them aflame
> In the grey of the dawn; and myself
> Will lay myself straight in my bed,
> And draw the sheet under my chin.

The combination of the image of coldness—making the body cold by bathing in ice water—and the image of diminishing natural light—closing the window shutters, lighting candles—effectively establishes a *pattern of death imagery.* The images are not complicated or obscure, nor are they developed extensively. In simple, direct, and chilling economy they create the precisely stark atmosphere of death.

Images, then, are discovered along the twin spectrums of difficulty and aesthetics. They induce us to make mental pictures of sadness, joy, jealousy, death, etc., and in all cases, they serve to advance basic mood and meaning in a dramatic, exciting way.

IRONY. When a poet, or a speaker in a poem, *says* one thing but means another, irony results. Furthermore, whenever there is a discernible difference between what is said and what is meant, or between what is *stated* and what is *implied,* irony results. In some instances the speaker is aware of the double meaning (what is said, what is meant), and in some instances he is not.

In plays, there is often a great deal of irony when a character does not grasp the significance of what he is saying or of his situation. In poetry, irony is used to make dramatic contrasts between appearances and reality and between belief and fact. Speakers in poems are often not allowed, by the poet, to show any deep understanding of their situations. In this way the poet allows the reader, aware of the discrepancy, to understand the speaker more fully. Sometimes a poet uses irony to show us imperfections and especially wry contradictions—a teacher cursing study or a priest acting sensually. The irony results from the difference between what *should be* and what actually *is.* When this kind of irony becomes very strong, it usually results in humor (and sometimes invective). Since irony expresses two things simultaneously, it is often used to convey the heart of paradoxical aspects of reality.

METAPHOR (see *figurative language,* pp. 38ff.).

PARADOX. Basically, paradox is the presentation of something which cannot be logically true. This is a poetic device which has recently become of great interest to literary critics, particularly to the so-called New Critics, and its use has frequently been noted as one of the distinguishing marks of a sophisticated poet. Paradox is the joining together of things which we would not at first think should be joined together, but which, on second thought, are obliquely appropriate in their conjunction.

A reader is often surprised by the basically curious and unexpected truth which a paradox crystallizes. His initial response to paradox is often simply, "How can this be?" The point is that the poet is intentionally making us ask this question, and by answering it we may discover much of the meaning of the poem. Cleanth Brooks and the New Critics view paradox as the poet's intentional "indirection" or subtle manner of making a point, as, for example, when Shakespeare writes: "When my love swears that she is made of truth/I do believe her, though I know she lies."

Sometimes a poem itself is a large *sustained paradox,* or, really, a *seeming* paradox. On further consideration, things thought to be paradoxical are, in fact, logical. Consider, for example, "Richard Cory," the well-known poem by E. A. Robinson (1869–1935):

> Whenever Richard Cory went down town,
> We people on the pavement looked at him:
> He was a gentleman from sole to crown,
> Clean favored, and imperially slim.
>
> And he was always quietly arrayed,
> And he was always human when he talked;
> But still he fluttered pulses when he said,
> "Good-morning," and he glittered when he walked.
>
> And he was rich—yes, richer than a king,
> And admirably schooled in every grace:
> In fine, we thought that he was everything
> To make us wish that we were in his place.
>
> So on we worked, and waited for the night,
> And went without the meat, and cursed the bread;
> And Richard Cory, one calm summer night,
> Went home and put a bullet through his head.

This poem is, really, an extended or sustained paradox. It at first seems grotesquely absurd that this fine gentleman, envied by everyone in town, could commit suicide. Notice that we write "seems," for, in fact, on second thought, the suicide becomes understandable. Richard Cory had not really been *known* by the people in town. He had only been seen superficially as a rich man. The townspeople did not know that rich people could suffer their private agonies, nor were they perceptive enough to sense Cory's basic alienation from society. There is heavy irony here, as for example when the speaker asserts, "we thought that he was everything/To make us wish that we were in his place." Tension is generated throughout the poem, and it culminates in suicide (the basic alienation behind the suicide was used as the poem's mainspring when set to music by folk-rock singers-composers Simon and Garfunkel).

Pathos. This is the quality which results when a reader feels strong sorrow or pity for the speaker or character in a poem. A poet creates pathos to win the reader's sympathy (and thus interest). Pathos can be an effective poetic device, because it establishes a close relationship with the reader. When one feels pity for the speaker in a poem, one is closer to the speaker and hence to the entire world which the poet is creating (and poets, generally, are interested in ways of bringing their readers into the worlds which poems create or reflect). When handled carefully, pathos can be extremely effective, as, for example, in "Patterns," a long poem by Amy Lowell (1874–1925). Here is the way it begins:

I walk down the garden paths,
And all the daffodils
Are blowing, and the bright blue squills.
I walk down the patterned garden-paths
In my stiff, brocaded gown.
With my powdered hair and jewelled fan,
I too am a rare
Pattern. As I wander down
The garden paths.

My dress is richly figured,
And the train
Makes a pink and silver stain
On the gravel, and the thrift
Of the borders.
Just a plate of current fashion,
Tripping by in high-heeled, ribboned shoes.
Not a softness anywhere about me,
Only whalebone and brocade.
And I sink on a seat in the shade
Of a lime tree. For my passion
Wars against the stiff brocade.
The daffodils and squills
Flutter in the breeze
As they please.
And I weep;
For the lime-tree is in blossom
And one small flower has dropped upon my bosom.

[For several long stanzas the speaker continues to comment on the *freedom* of nature around her, contrasting it with *her* feelings of being *imprisoned;* she pulls out a letter which informs her that her husband has just died in action. Our *pity* continues to increase gradually. The last stanza follows.]

> In Summer and in Winter I shall walk
> Up and down
> The patterned garden-paths
> In my stiff, brocaded gown.
> The squills and daffodils
> Will give place to pillared roses, and to asters, and to snow.
> I shall go
> Up and down,
> In my gown.
> Gorgeously arrayed,
> Boned and stayed.
> And the softness of my body will be guarded from embrace
> By each button, hook, and lace.
> For the man who should loose me is dead,
> Fighting with the Duke in Flanders,
> In a pattern called a war.
> Christ! What are patterns for?

In this poem Amy Lowell carefully gains our sympathy by beginning with, and sustaining, a contrast between the stiff, imprisoning clothing of the woman speaking and the freedom of movement enjoyed by the flowers in her garden, and then moving to a greater kind of imprisonment. By the time we hear of her main unhappiness, we feel entirely sympathetic; our involvement in the poem is steadily deepened.

Sometimes, incidentally, pathos is overdone. The result is *bathos,* a kind of extreme or insincere pathos (bathos can also mean an anticlimax, or sudden descent from an elevated plane).

PERSONIFICATION. This is the device of writing about things and ideas which are abstract or inanimate as if they were human persons. When a poet refers to Mother Earth or to Beauty as a girl, he is personifying them, assigning them animate, human existence. When an abstraction becomes a person, a poem acquires a heightened dramatic relevance, as, for example, in the opening lines of Emily Dickinson's poem in which Death arrives in his chariot to take the speaker: "Because I could not stop for Death,/He kindly stopped for me." Sometimes an entire poem is based on one or more personifications, as, for instance, in a poem entitled "The Flesh and the Spirit" by Anne Bradstreet (1612?–1672), in which the two title subjects are presented as a pair of sisters engaged in a dialogue. The poem opens in this way:

> In secret place where once I stood,
> Close by the banks of lacrym flood,
> I heard two sisters reason on
> Things that are past, and things to come.
> One Flesh was called, who had her eye
> On worldly wealth and vanity;
> The other Spirit, who did rear
> Her thoughts unto a higher sphere.

When personifications assume major roles in a poem, as they do in Anne Bradstreet's, we are involved in *allegory*, a complicated structural device in certain poems, plays, and novels in which the characters are personifications of abstract qualities. For example, in Spenser's *The Fairie Queene* there is a good account of the seven deadly sins. Each sin has a particular personality, behaves in a certain way, has basic human characteristics, and rides an animal which mirrors them. Here is Spenser's three-stanza personification of Gluttony:

> And by his side rode loathsome Gluttony,
> Deforméd creature, on a filthie swyne,
> His belly was upblowne with luxury,
> And eke with fatnesse swollen were his eyne,
> And like a Crane his necke was long and fyne,
> With which he swallowed up excessive feast,
> For want whereof poore people oft did pyne;
> And all the way, most like a brutish beast,
> He spuéd up his gorge, that all did him deteast.
>
> In greene vine leaves he was right fitly clad;
> For other clothes he could not weare for heat,

And on his head an yvie girland had,
From under which fast trickled downe the sweat:
Still as he rode, he somewhat still did eat,
And in his hand did beare a bouzing can,
Of which he supt so oft, that on his seat
His dronken corse he scarse upholden can:
In shape and life more like a monster, then a man.

Unfit he was for any worldly thing,
And eke unhable once to stirre or go,
Nor meet to be of counsell to a king,
Whose mind in meat and drinke was drownéd so,
That from his frend he seldome knew his fo:
Full of diseases was his carcas blew,
And a dry dropsie through his flesh did flow,
Which by misdiet daily greater grew:
Such one was Gluttony, the second of that crew.

This intentionally unappetizing portrait is effective as a means of making the sin of gluttony dramatically visual. The device of personification has been used as a good alternative to direct description.

Poetic Diction. The words which a poet chooses constitute his *diction.* The term "poetic diction" applies both to the diction of all poets, and, in some circles, to that language in poetry which seems *self-consciously* "poetic." (When a poet tries too hard to achieve a "poetic diction," the phrase has a pejorative sense, sometimes known as *peri-phrasis.*) It should be clear that the kinds of words a poet (or dramatist, or fiction writer) uses constitutes a large—perhaps the largest—aspect of his style. There is no single rule about diction in poetry. A very *unfanciful* poem like Cummings' "I Sing of Olaf" makes special use of poetic diction, while the fanciful "The Hunting of the Snark" does not. Some poets, like Robert Frost, achieve dynamic mood and effectively present meaning through colloquial language. They fashion poems from the language of everyday speech and the basic speech patterns of ordinary people. The Frost poem which usually opens editions of his poems is written in very colloquial language:

THE PASTURE

I'm going out to clean the pasture spring;
I'll only stop to rake the leaves away
(And wait to watch the water clear, I may):
I sha'n't be gone long.—You come too.

I'm going out to fetch the little calf
That's standing by the mother. It's so young,
It totters when she licks it with her tongue.
I sha'n't be gone long.—You come too.

By using this kind of friendly, familiar language, Frost hopes to establish a close relationship with his readers. The diction puts the reader at ease. Compare the more self-conscious diction in the opening of "Ode to a Nightingale" by John Keats (1795–1821):

My heart aches, and a drowsy numbness pains
  My sense, as though of hemlock I had drunk,
Or emptied some dull opiate to the drains
  One minute past, and Lethe-wards had sunk:
'Tis not through envy of thy happy lot,
  But being too happy in thine happiness—
    That thou, light-wingèd Dryad of the trees,
      In some melodious plot
  Of beechen green, and shadows numberless,
    Singest of summer in full-throated ease.

The ordinary person simply does not think of hemlock, Lethe, or Dryad. The diction is intentionally fanciful and "poetic."

A poet does not simply decide whether to use figurative or literal language. He also decides from where along the spectrum of poetic diction he wants to choose his basic vocabulary. Diction, it should be pointed out, is not connected to the degree of complexity of meaning. A poet can be very complex using ordinary speech, as Wallace Stevens (1879–1956) demonstrates in his poem "Anecdote of the Jar," or very simple and straightforward while using fanciful speech, as in Keats' "To One Who Has

Been Long in the City Pent." Finally, it should be noted that many poets enjoy mixing up the kinds of diction within a poem, shifting from a colloquial line or stanza to a formal one, or, perhaps, from stark to flowery language, in order to startle us or to create subdivisions within the poem. Shifts in diction generate shifts in tone, and thus diction is in itself a method of organization.

POINT OF VIEW. When we read a poem we are listening not simply to a poet, but to a particular *speaker*. Sometimes, of course, the poet and the speaker are one (as in love sonnets in which Shakespeare or Elizabeth Browning, for example, apparently speak to particular people while at the same time make universally felt recordings of the feelings of love). In general, however, we should discuss the speaker, or "voice," in a poem as if he were someone distinct and separate from the poet. Sometimes we describe this speaker as the *mask* or the *persona* of the poem, that is, the mask which the poet assumes when he writes his poem. The poet, in other words, often acquires a new identity when he writes as a successful man, an unrequited lover, a young girl, and so forth. In each poem the speaker is identified not simply by what he says, but by the words he uses and by the way he responds to his situation. Persona, as a device, enables a poet to create whatever point of view he wishes. He can tell us his ideas about love, for example, *from the point of view* of one who loves futilely, successfully, ardently, or quietly.

By dramatizing the point of view, a poet increases the effectiveness of his poem. In the following short poem by Thomas Lovell Beddoes (1803–1849), the speaker appears to us as one who is tired, busy, and anxious for death. The speaker, as far as we can tell, is not the same person as the poet:

IF THERE WERE DREAMS TO SELL

If there were dreams to sell,
  What would you buy?
Some cost a passing bell;
  Some a light sigh,

That shakes from Life's fresh crown
Only a rose-leaf down
If there were dreams to sell,
Merry and sad to tell,
And the crier rang the bell,
  What would you buy?

A cottage lone and still,
  With bowers nigh,
Shadowy, my woes to still,
  Until I die.
Such pearl from life's fresh crown
Fain would I shake me down.
Were dreams to have at will,
This would best heal my ill,
  This would I buy.

It is also possible that the poet planned the voice of the first stanza to be different from the voice of the second stanza; that is, one voice asks the question—what dream would you buy if dreams were for sale?—and a second voice answers that he, *for one,* would buy a lone cottage, and so forth. In any event, the poem is intentionally designed to ask the *reader* to consider what dreams *he* would buy. We are given *an* answer—not necessarily the poet's personal answer—with which we can compare our own.

Often a voice in a poem becomes universalized by the poet. If you recall Robert Frost's "The Road Not Taken," you will notice that the poem is told from the point of view of *a* person (*any* person) who took the road "less traveled by." It *might* apply to Frost himself, but it does not have to. We are primarily concerned with defining the point of view. When we write about a poem *we try to characterize the speaker whose voice we hear.* Sometimes, of course, the speaker and the poet will obviously be the same, as, for example, in the blind Milton's sonnet on his blindness. A large body of literary criticism has been developed in order to help differentiate *Chaucer the narrator* of the *Canterbury Tales* (that is, Chaucer the pilgrim in a company of other pilgrims) from *Chaucer the poet.*

SETTING. A poet creates a setting for his poem by choosing details which effectively characterize the time and place of the action. With virtually Faustian power, the poet is able to shape his setting to the exact needs of his poetic world and purpose. While setting sometimes arises automatically from the circumstances of composition, it is more often strictly the result of the poet's private imagination. The scene in which a poem is set often becomes an important part of the poem's meaning. We can all think of numerous poems which dramatically make the setting the lion's share of their impact—poems like Milton's "Ode on the Morning of Christ's Nativity," Wordsworth's "Daffodils," and Robert Frost's "Stopping by Woods on a Snowy Evening."

What Kinds of Poems Are There?

Genre

Works of literature belong to particular families or *genres*. Each genre has basic characteristics, as well as a "tradition" or historical development *as a genre*. When a poet composes an *elegy*, for example, he is writing within the *elegiac tradition*, and his poem will follow certain definite *conventions*.

A convention (from the Latin *convenire*, to come together, to agree) is something about which we have all come to agree. A *literary convention*, then, is any device pertaining to values or methods which we recognize as recurring in certain kinds of poems.

While a genre is a kind of poetry—epic, elegy, epithalamion, etc.—a convention is only a *feature* of a certain genre, and not a genre in itself. A convention makes a poem more specialized and thus enables it to be more particularly classified. A convention is a rule which the writer and his readers agree upon; the poet will do certain things in a certain way and will be able to know that his audience will recognize that he is using a convention. Thus, a convention frees the writer from having constantly to overexplain what he is doing; however, a convention also limits a poet, because it dictates that he *has* to do certain things. Readers who are not familiar with certain conventions may, it follows, misinterpret a poem. Certain genres are based upon adherence to certain conventions. Greek tragedies must follow certain rules; so too must sonnets and epics. When we write about literature, we need to classify the work in question to the greatest extent possible, for in classification lies clarification. When we know precisely what a poet is trying to do, we can better decide whether he is succeeding. Distinctions between genres, or kinds, of literature, are fairly clear, though sometimes a poet departs from ("breaks with") tradition to try something new and different. Such departures from tradition represent part of the lifeblood of poetry.

The oldest generic grouping divides all literature into three classes—*drama, epic,* and *lyric.* Drama has reference to speeches and actions of characters on a stage. Within drama there are of course various subdivisions (tragedy, comedy, etc.), which are discussed in Part II of this book. *Epic* refers to long narrative poems such as the *Iliad,* the *Odyssey, Beowulf,* and *Paradise Lost.* Epic, longer than the drama, was originally intended to be chanted before an audience. Lengthy narrative has been divided into various particular genres (romance, novel, etc.), and we will discuss some of the major narrative traditions, stemming from epic, in Part III of this book.

Our immediate concern is with lyric (a term used to describe the "poems" which were accompanied by music played on a *lyre*). From this basic ancient genre spring most of the "kinds" of poetry with which we need to be familiar. The lyric was always shorter than both the drama and the epic, just as poems today are generally—though not necessarily—shorter than plays and novels. Tragedy and epic have been inclined toward using stories provided by both myth and history. Lyric, being shorter, generally accomplishes more in less time. Poetry, deriving from the lyric genre, tends, therefore, to be more compressed or distilled. A poet generally makes his points more economically than either the dramatist or novelist. Lyric is more likely to be fashioned out of individual mood and imagination (though there are, of course, many instances of poetry being fashioned out of myth or history). Nevertheless, the experience recorded in poetry is usually of a more personal nature, for basically lyric was, and is, a genre of self-expression.

Genres of literature have various differences which will be made apparent as we survey some of the basic conventions as well as the minor classifications within each group. Each large section of this book corresponds to one of the three ancient genres, poetry to lyric, prose to epic, and drama to drama. At this point we are ready to survey some of the basic classifications of poetry.

Basic Kinds of Poems

ELEGY. One particular kind of lyric is the *elegy*, a poem in which the speaker either mourns for someone who has died or contemplates the tragic import of death. The feeling of loss is usually mitigated by a final, restorative optimism generated by the discovery of some happier enduring principle which transcends the particular tragedy (death is only the beginning of a new and better life, for example). The poet traditionally introduces various mythological or classical characters who arrive to mourn with the poet. Often abstract personifications are introduced. In the *pastoral elegy*, shepherds—along with mythological characters—and nymphs are introduced in order to aid the speaker in his mourning. The extent to which a poet includes characters in his elegy is entirely arbitrary. So, too, is the length of the elegy. In the following short "Elegy," Lord Byron laments, characteristically, the death of a young person, and introduces Sorrow *personified* (see *personification*, pp. 48ff.), her head bowed in mourning near a gushing stream:

O snatch'd away in beauty's bloom!
On thee shall press no ponderous tomb;
  But on thy turf shall roses rear
  Their leaves, the earliest of the year,
And the wild cypress wave in tender gloom:

And oft by yon blue gushing stream
  Shall sorrow lean her drooping head,
And feed deep thought with many a dream,
  And lingering pause and lightly tread;
Fond wretch! as if her step disturb'd the dead!

Away! we know that tears are vain,
  That Death nor heeds nor hears distress:
Will this unteach us to complain?
  Or make one mourner weep the less?
And thou, who tell'st me to forget,
Thy looks are wan, thine eyes are wet.

In "Lycidas," the most celebrated *pastoral elegy* in English, Milton mourns the death of his young friend Edward King (who becomes a symbol of all promising men who die in their youth). King is depicted as a young shepherd-poet whose death is mourned by the other shepherds who will miss him, and his poetry, very much. The poem is long (193 lines) and filled with a number of complexities which scholars have been trying to clarify for many years. The following passage suggests the way in which Milton tries to depict the loss the shepherds feel for their friend the shepherd-poet:

But O the heavy change, now thou art gone,
Thee Shepherd, thee the Woods, and desert Caves,
With wild Thyme, and the gadding Vine o'ergrown,
And all their echoes mourn.
The Willows and the Hazel Copses green
Shall now no more be seen,
Fanning their joyous Leaves to thy soft lays.
As killing as the Canker to the Rose,
Or Taint-worm to the weanling Herds that graze,
Or Frost to Flowers, that their gay wardrobe wear,
When first the White-thorn blows;
Such, *Lycidas,* thy loss to Shepherd's ear.

The air of mourning ("the heavy change, now thou art gone")

surrounding the countryside is made explicitly pastoral through references to shepherds, plants, and green copses.

When an elegy is extremely formal or written as a definite chant, it is often referred to as a *threnody*, as Emerson's "Threnody on His Young Son." When an elegy is extremely simple, or a rather stark, unembellished statement of grief, it is sometimes referred to as a *dirge*. (The dirge, unlike the elegy, contains no attempt at positive consolation, for it is traditionally sung for the dead, instead of as a form of comfort for the living.)

ODE. An ode is a formal celebration of a special event and thus is usually a fairly public and ceremonious form of expression. However, poets have, over the years, written odes on a variety of subjects—as suggested by the titles of Thomas Gray's "Ode on the Pleasure Arising from Vicissitude" and Thomas Campbell's "Ode to Winter." In each case, however, the essential note of celebration is maintained.

Odes are usually one of three kinds: *Pindaric, Horatian,* and something resembling an "I want to call my poem an ode" variety. That is, some poets (including Keats, the author of some of the best so-called "odes" in the English language) call their poems "odes" even though they do not, strictly speaking, conform to accepted rules pertaining to the ode.

Horatian odes (after the Roman lyric poet and satirist Horace, 65–8 B.C.) are generally "quieter," more contemplative, and less irregular in their stanzaic structure or verse form than *Pindaric odes* (after the Greek poet Pindar, 522?–443? B.C.). The Pindaric ode, attempted by Ben Jonson, Thomas Gray, and numerous other poets, consists of *strophe, antistrophe,* and *epode,* corresponding to the chorus' turning one way, back again, and then not moving at all (as it recited the different parts of the ode). Pindar's stanzas varied a great deal, and English poets have more or less equated "Pindaric" with stanzaic chaos (when it is intentional, of course). Wordsworth, for example, varies both line length and stanza length in his famous "Ode in Intimations of Immortality." Horatian odes, most obviously represented by Andrew Marvell's "Horatian Ode Upon Cromwell's Return from Ireland," in contrast to the Pindaric odes, have regularity of stanza, verse, and form.

Modern readers of poetry have little interest in the technical problems and aspects of odes, though occasionally they are genuinely surprised by the startling effectiveness of irregularity when they encounter it, for example, in an exciting poem like Dryden's "A Song for St. Cecilia's Day," a modified Pindaric ode. Five years before Dryden wrote this ode there had been established by a London musical society a custom of celebrating November 22 as the feast of St. Cecilia (the patroness of music). In Dryden's ode, different instruments are summoned forth to produce sharply contrasting musical sounds. The variation of stanzaic and line length adds a great deal. Consider, for example, the third and fourth stanzas of Dryden's ode:

– III –

The trumpet's loud clangor
Excites us to arms,
With shrill notes of anger,
And mortal alarms.
The double double double beat
Of the thund-ring Drum
Cries: "Hark! the foes come;
Charge, charge, 't is too late to retreat."

– IV –

The soft complaining Flute
In dying notes discovers
The woes of helpless lovers,
Whose dirge is whisper'd by the warbling Lute.

Sonnet. As we discussed in the versification section, a sonnet is a fourteen-line poem in iambic pentameter. This short lyric form has been popular since it was imported from Italy by the Earl of Surrey. In the late sixteenth and early seventeenth centuries it became "fashionable" for a poet to write a sequence, or series, of sonnets on a particular theme. Such series were known as *sonnet cycles,* and among the better known ones are those which were written by Sidney, Spenser, Daniel, and Shakespeare. The main reason that this short lyric form—perhaps as close to the original idea of "lyric" as any existing form—has been so widely experimented with is that it forces the poet to crystallize his ideas, to compress his thoughts on a subject into fourteen lines. However, as the development of the sonnet cycle suggests, a poet often felt that it would be impossible to express satisfactorily a woman's beauty or the mysteries of love in fourteen lines!

EPITHALAMION. This curious kind of poem, probably first used as a literary form by the Greek lyric poetess Sappho (620?–565? B.C.), is very specialized, for it pertains only to the celebration of marriage and is thus specifically composed to be sung outside the bridal chamber on the wedding night. Often personifications or classical and mythological characters are introduced, as in the famous epithalamion Spenser wrote for his own wedding. The seventeenth century revived the epithalamion as a literary form, and a large number of poets experimented with it (Spenser, Sidney, Donne, Jonson, Herrick, Crashaw, Marvell, Dryden).

BALLAD, OR STORY-SONG. A ballad is a short song usually transmitted orally which deals with simple folk stories, either of characters, events, or battles. A ballad thus operates on a relatively "low" or realistic poetic level. The ballad usually makes use of *refrains* primarily because they were originally sung or recited and the words became dramatically effective through repetition. Ballads have a very pronounced metrical pattern, or system of stress (see *rhyme*, p. 20), and often use a line with four beats (stressed sounds), but with any number of unstressed syllables. Keats' mysterious ballad "La Belle Dame Sans Merci" has enchanted an untold number of readers and, although it is relatively long, it is worthy of being presented in full:

"O what can ail thee, Knight-at-arms,
  Alone and palely loitering?
The sedge has wither'd from the Lake,
  And no birds sing.

"O what can ail thee, Knight-at-arms!
  So haggard and so woebegone?
The squirrel's granary is full,
  And the harvest's done.

"I see a lily on thy brow
  With anguish moist and fever dew,
And on thy cheeks a fading rose
  Fast withereth too.

"I met a Lady in the Meads,
  Full beautiful—a fairy's child,
Her hair was long, her foot was light,
  And her eyes were wild.

"I made a Garland for her head,
  And bracelets too, and fragrant Zone;
She look'd at me as she did love,
  And made sweet moan.

"I set her on my pacing steed
  And nothing else saw all day long,
For sidelong would she bend and sing
  A fairy's song.

"She found me roots of relish sweet,
  And honey wild, and manna dew,
And sure in language strange she said
  'I love thee true.'

"She took me to her elfin grot
  And there she wept and sigh'd full sore,
And there I shut her wild wild eyes
  With kisses four.

"And there she lulléd me asleep,
  And there I dream'd—Ah! Woe betide!
The latest dream I ever dream'd
  On the cold hill side.

"I saw pale Kings and Princes too,
  Pale warriors, death-pale were they all;
They cried—'La belle Dame sans Merci
  Thee hath in thrall.'

"I saw their starved lips in the gloam
With horrid warning gapéd wide,
And I awoke and found me here
On the cold hill's side.

"And this is why I sojourn here
Alone and palely loitering,
Though the sedge is wither'd from the Lake
And no birds sing."

SHORT LYRIC. Some short poems are simply known as *lyrics*. In general a lyric is a short poem, often of a very musical quality, in which the poet expresses a private feeling. A lyric is emotional and individual. The subject matter can be anything at all. The poem can be any length and in any form, though generally the length is short and the form simple. In a lyric the poet usually attempts to capture one idea, or one frame of mind, as, for example, in Robert Browning's attempt to give us the exuberance of a young girl in springtime:

IPPA'S SONG

The year's at the spring,
And day's at the morn;
Morning's at seven;
The hill-side's dew-pearl'd;
The lark's on the wing;
The snail's on the thorn;
God's in His heaven—
All's right with the world!

While a lyric is named after the broad genre "lyric," it does not have any particular closeness to the large genre; the names happen to be the same, but lyric poetry does not have some sort of franchise on the properties of "lyric" as it was anciently understood. Lyrics tend to provide readers with a certain amount of emotional satisfaction, primarily because they tend to crystallize, or distill, a particular moment or singular feeling. In its simplicity a lyric tends to teach us about looking at the world, and, particularly, at beautiful things. But beauty does not imply happiness in all cases; death is often celebrated in short lyrics, as, for example, in Tennyson's lyric poem "Break, Break, Break," in which he is lamenting the death of his friend Arthur Hallam (for whom Tennyson also wrote the long poem *In Memoriam*). In this short lyric, the musical quality is there, as is the sense of individual expression and of an emotionally charged condition, but the poem nevertheless is about death and focuses on the sense of loss which the poet feels now that his friend has died:

> Break, break, break,
> On thy cold grey stones, O Sea!
> And I would that my tongue could utter
> The thoughts that arise in me.
>
> O, well for the fisherman's boy,
> That he shouts with his sister at play!
> O, well for the sailor lad,
> That he sings in his boat on the bay!
>
> And the stately ships go on
> To their haven under the hill;
> But O for the touch of a vanished hand,
> And the sound of a voice that is still!
>
> Break, break, break,
> At the foot of thy crags, O Sea!
> But the tender grace of a day that is dead
> Will never come back to me.

Lyrics reflect the musical origins of poetry as it was sung, chanted, and recited. The "lyric" came to be considered a poem that was to be sung, and in the sixteenth and seventeenth centuries numerous poems were simply entitled "songs," and, carelessly, were not even differentiated from the more formal songs designed for musical accompaniment. Critics agree that musical qualities are often maintained—but not essentially so—in lyric poems. A lyric, in its brevity and self-expression, is perhaps best described in Schopenhauer's words, "the utterance that is overheard."

BURLESQUE POETRY. Burlesque poetry has its origins in the classical Greek comedies of Aristophanes (448?–380? B.C.) and was advanced significantly as a genre during the Middle Ages, particularly by Chaucer in some of his *Canterbury Tales.* While *parody* tends to satirize individual poets' styles and methods, burlesque is broader and usually makes fun of large genres and conventions (as well as entire writing styles). For example, there are some good burlesques of *carpe diem* (see pp. 73ff.). Chaucer convincingly satirizes the conventions of medieval romance in "The Nun's Priest's Tale."

The term "burlesque" acquired new meaning in about 1650 with the appearance of critical discussions of *Scarronesque* poetry (based on the ideas of the French satirist Paul Scarron, 1610–1660); the focal point of this kind of burlesque was the substitution of bourgeois for aristocratic manners. In the eighteenth century poets began to write *mock-heroic* poetry in couplets (a practice begun earlier by the satirist Samuel Butler, 1612–1680, in his *Hudibras*), and Pope's *Dunciad* was typical. In these mock-heroic poems—so named because they treated as heroic people and events which quite obviously were *not* heroic—the targets were other poets' styles, the age's social manners and attitudes, which the authors felt to be in need of reform, rival poets, and sometimes religious practices or political beliefs.

In the twentieth century there has been a notable absence of burlesque poetry, probably because the major burlesque efforts have gone into plays for the stage (in the tradition of burlesque drama as it first entered into English literature through John Gay's satire of Italian opera, *The Beggar's Opera,* and as it was advanced in the nineteenth century by the opera-burlesques of Gilbert and Sullivan).

Mock-heroic, sometimes called mock-epic, is a complex and subtle kind of poetry. It is difficult to treat characters and situations more seriously than they merit and this is the precise mainspring of mock-heroic, making serious and lofty those matters, events, people, and situations which are, in reality, extremely trivial and dull. The best example in English poetry is probably

Pope's *The Rape of The Lock* in which the snipping off of a girl's hair is narrated in epic terms and treated as an event of epic significance. There are epic battles, references to national feelings, consolation and reward for great efforts, and so forth. These devices commonly associated with the heroic genre tend to *inflate* the material and thereby render it, in its disproportion, extremely hilarious.

In contrast to mock-heroic poetry, a kind of poetry which makes things ridiculous by *inflating* them beyond true proportion, *travesty* directly *deflates* or minimizes things. For satiric purposes, travesty accomplishes virtually the same thing as mock-heroic, making fun of ideas, people, writing styles, and social and religious institutions and practices. Travesty, however, treats things as if they were *less* important than they actually are (and thus, as a poetic method, is the reverse of mock-heroic). In Dryden's *Mac Flecknoe*, for example, the title character departs from this world not by rising to heaven, but by falling through a trap door.

All in all, burlesque literature—including satiric opera, mock-heroic, parody, and travesty—is a delicate genre and difficult to control. Because people like to laugh, the genre will never vanish; however, because tonal decisions and choices of details have to be so exact to be truly funny, the genre—or whole category of burlesque—will remain complex.

FABLE. A fable is a tale which employs animals as the principal characters. Fable supposedly originated in a primitive kind of *allegory*, literature in which events and characters beyond those actually mentioned are present either by implication or symbolically. Fable, as well as myth, relates to allegory because animals are, in effect, used allegorically to convey basic moral meanings important for human development.

The first formally collected fables, those assembled by Aesop in the sixth century B.C., had brief moral messages presented through the medium of direct and sometimes dry verse. The fable is an important literary genre, because it is a good vehicle for indirectly attacking ideas, institutions, beliefs, or personal enemies. As a form of satire, fable was wrought into a fuller kind of poetry by the Frenchman Jean de La Fontaine (1621–

1695), who, using irony and drama, wrote fables in the form of lyric poetry.

The fable has always been considered a starkly realistic genre which can be written in either prose or poetry. The main idea is simply to use animals instead of people with the purpose of making, in an entertaining way, a dramatic point (moral) about *human* conduct and resources. One of La Fontaine's fables, for example, is about a fly which, as she buzzes busily around six horses pulling a coach up a hill, sincerely feels that she alone is responsible for getting the coach up the hill. While La Fontaine refers directly only to this silly fly, it is obvious to his audience that his point is really about people, and in particular about the type of feminine busybody who buzzes around others and who, convinced of her own self-importance, thinks that she is the pillar of the community—when in fact she contributes nothing.

The *beast epic,* incidentally, not to be confused with a (beast) fable, is a long tale written in epic style. A good example is Pierre de Saint-Cloud's twelfth-century *Roman de Renart* in which animals become knights on horses, and their lairs become castles. A highly specialized motif, the beast epic does not appear with much frequency.

PASTORAL. As we mentioned before, an *elegy* sometimes makes use of shepherds, woodlands, sheep, flowers, etc., and thereby becomes a *pastoral* elegy. *Pastoral* poetry is in itself an entire genre or kind of poetry which has enjoyed considerable popularity for over 2,000 years. Poets have frequently experienced a generalized kinship with the quiet existence of shepherds and have tended, therefore, to use and idealize it in verse. Pastoral (from the Latin word for shepherd, *pastor*) poetry derives its essence from setting—always rural, always inhabited by shepherds, shepherdesses, and, less importantly, by sheep! The shepherds are usually thoughtful, sensitive, aesthetic, quiet, and in love. They spend their hours combining the care of their flocks with philosophical discussions of life, death, and love. Their life is idealized by poets, and thus there are never real dangers or hardships to threaten them. Sometimes they engage in singing matches which are self-consciously "literary," as, for example, many of the songs which are interspersed throughout Sir Philip Sidney's long pastoral prose romance *Arcadia.* Ordinary rural life, with its attendant hardships, is never seen. Instead, everything is romanticized. The basic simplicity of thought and setting tends to make pastoral poetry immediately acceptable to most readers, though a few (like Dr. Samuel Johnson) balk at its lack of realism, while others complain bitterly of its basic silliness and lack of relevance.

There are subdivisions within the genre of pastoral poetry. For example, in one kind of pastoral poem, a lovesick shepherd sings what is known as a *love lament;* singing of a beloved one's death becomes a *pastoral elegy* (see *pastoral elegy,* p. 56); singing of friends under disguised names becomes *pastoral allegory.* Many pastoral poems, furthermore, are simply called *idylls.* An idyll is any short poem (and, actually, any prose composition) which concentrates on the pleasures and beauties of rustic life. *Pastoral,* as a literary term, can be applied to all basic kinds of literature, and thus there are *pastoral romances* in prose and also *pastoral dramas* which have essentially the same setting and characters as pastoral poems.

The shepherds of pastoral poetry usually exist in the Golden Age, a world in time uncomplicated by trouble, war, or hardship, and, indeed, many pastoral poems are written as nostalgic reflections looking back to a world which was better than those in which the poets live. In pastoral poems a shepherd generally sits beneath a tree in a mountainside vale; he sings and plays his "pipe" (flute) while the sun shines down its golden rays on him; the following opening of an anonymous pastoral love lament is typical:

> While that the sun with his beams hot
>   Scorched the fruits in vale and mountain,
> Philon the shepherd, late forgot,
>   Sitting beside a crystal fountain,
>   In shadow of a green oak tree
>   Upon his pipe this song played he:
> Adieu Love, adieu Love, untrue Love,
> Untrue Love, untrue Love, adieu Love;
> Your mind is light, soon lost for new love.

In short, in most pastoral poems, to borrow from Milton's

"L'Allegro," "every shepherd tells his tale/Under the hawthorn in the dale." And shepherds, as William Blake aptly summarized, go "Piping down the valleys wild,/Piping songs of pleasant glee."

MADRIGAL. A madrigal is a short song, used originally in Northern Italy, which gained great popularity with sixteenth- and seventeenth-century poets. Madrigals are written in various metrical forms. In early madrigals several tercets were followed by one or two rhyming couplets. However, there has been sufficient experimentation with the genre to accept the term "madrigal" as meaning any short song—as, for example, the following song by Shakespeare entitled "Madrigal":

> Crabbed Age and Youth
> Cannot live together:
> Youth is full of pleasure,
> Age is full of care;
> Youth like summer morn,
> Age like winter weather,
> Youth like summer brave,
> Age like winter bare:
> Youth is full of sport,
> Age's breath is short,
> Youth is simple, Age is lame!
> Youth is hot and bold,
> Age is weak and cold,
> Youth is wild, and Age is tame:—
> Age, I do abhor thee,
> Youth, I do adore thee;
> O! my Love, my Love is young!
> Age, I do defy thee—
> O sweet shepherd, hie thee—
> For methinks thou stay'st too long.

The ending of this pastoral madrigal (and most madrigals *are* pastoral), in which the poet tells the shepherd to conclude this debate before he becomes boring, is very humorous.

MONOLOGUE. A monologue is a speech in any kind of literature which is delivered by one person. A play contains a monologue whenever one character steps forward to speak by himself

—and in prolonged form this kind of monologue is usually considered a *soliloquy* (NB: *colloquy*—two speakers). Poets often allow the speaker to deliver a long, personal, dramatic speech, presuming a particular audience, or pretending that there is no audience (to suggest, thereby, that the speaker is simply being overheard while talking to himself).

In English poetry, the *dramatic monologue* was primarily developed by Robert Browning in long poems like "My Last Duchess." Since Browning's efforts, there have been many excellent dramatic monologues in poetry, from Tennyson's "Ulysses" to T. S. Eliot's "The Love Song of J. Alfred Prufrock." Robert Frost has also written some excellent dramatic monologues, using as his solitary speakers various "Yankee" characters from New England farmlands.

DOGGEREL. Doggerel is a kind of poetry which might almost be termed "nonpoetry," for it is *badly* written verse. Doggerel, characterized by monotonous and dull rhymes and trivial subject matter, is often intentionally satirical. Doggerel is frequently used *deliberately* as a technical means of conveying burlesque as in Samuel Butler's *Hudibras.*

VERSE EPISTLE. This is a particular kind of *poem written as a letter,* usually to a friend or patron. There are two kinds of verse epistles: those derived from the *Epistles* of Horace and dealing mainly with philosophical problems, and those deriving from Ovid's *Heroides* and dealing mainly with romantic subjects. The Horatian variety has enjoyed the greatest popularity. While not, generally speaking, a particularly exciting or unusual kind of poetry, verse epistles have been effectively written by many good poets, particularly by Alexander Pope in his *Moral Essays* and also in his well-known *Epistle to Dr. Arbuthnot.* Dryden also used the form quite well, writing—like Pope, in couplets—such frequently anthologized verse epistles as "To My Dear Friend, Mr. Congreve" and "To Sir Godfrey Kneller, Principal Painter to His Majesty."

FOLK SONG. A folk song is a lyric which has its origins not in the individual imagination, but rather in a collective oral tradition. That is, a folk song is a lyric which has been fashioned, preserved, and transmitted orally rather than through written words. A folk song, then, is quite literally a song rather than a poem. Nevertheless, a number of English poets have written poems which are either similar to, or nearly the same as, the popular folk songs from which they are derived. There are thousands upon thousands of sea chanties, working songs, ballads, and lullabies which have never been put into words on paper. There are, however, many folk ballads which *have* been written down, particularly, for example, the Scottish folk lyrics written by Robert Burns (1759–1796). The following folk-song-turned-into-ballad is perhaps his best known:

O my Luve's like a red, red rose
  That's newly sprung in June:
O my Luve's like the melodie
  That's sweetly play'd in tune.

As fair art thou, my bonnie lass,
  So deep in luve am I:
And I will luve thee still, my dear,
  Till a' the seas gang dry:

Till a' the seas gang dry, my dear,
  And the rocks melt w'the sun;
I will luve thee still, my dear,
  While the sands o' life shall run.

And fare thee weel, my only Luve!
  And fare thee weel a while!
And I will come again, my Luve,
  Tho' it were ten thousand mile.

While many folk songs have dealt with love, and while the bulk of English poems which have the *qualities* of folk songs have been about love, they have, in more recent times, become more expressly sociological and political, dealing more often with varieties of injustice rather than varieties of love.

FREE VERSE (VERS LIBRE). Free verse is an experimental response to metrical regularity. The substitution of rhythm for metrical regularity makes a good deal of Ezra Pound's poetry free verse. It is still a point of critical debate whether the use of rhythm is, in itself, sufficient to transform prose into poetry. Some critics argue that the use of rhythm is, by itself, sufficient to make words into poetry, while other critics argue that the use of rhythm instead of meter can result only in prose (in a technical sense). There are, certainly, historical antecedents behind the twentieth-century popularity of free verse experimentation. Milton, for example, wrote a good deal of free verse, though he didn't call it that, as, for example, in some of his *metrically irregular* passages in *Samson Agonistes*. The list of other experimenters is virtually endless, and, in the twentieth century, free verse has become more common than formal verse. Rilke, Eliot, and Pound have all written free verse, feeling that in many ways it is more "natural" than the formal regularity of traditional verse patterns. Free verse, by definition, is in a constant state of becoming. A great deal of creative and exciting experimentation is currently taking place. Attempting to make descriptions more natural, free verse sets as its goal the substitution of an inner rhythm, or cadence of *thought*, for the often wooden, self-conscious rhythm of regular poetic feet and recurring rhyme. The following lines by Whitman display the rhythm that can be generated without metrical regularity:

> A child said *What is the grass?* fetching it to me with full hands;
> How could I answer the child? I do not know what it is any more than he.
>
> I guess it must be the flag of my disposition, out of hopeful green stuff woven.
>
> Or I guess it is the handkerchief of the Lord,
> A scented gift and remembrancer designedly dropt,
> Bearing the owner's name someway in the corners, that we may see and remark, and say *Whose?*

In free verse of his own, Ezra Pound has acknowledged Whitman's creative innovation:

A PACT

I make a pact with you, Walt Whitman—
I have detested you long enough.
I come to you as a grown child
Who has had a pig-headed father;
I am old enough now to make friends.
It was you that broke the new wood,
Now is a time for carving.
We have one sap and one root—
Let there be commerce between us.

NARRATIVE POETRY. A narrative poem tells a story, and is basically, therefore, a cross between the major genres of lyric and epic. *Epic* and *ballad* are the two main kinds of narrative verse, and both are steeped in the *oral tradition* of literature. Story-telling in verse is entertainment for a particular audience, and usually for a large one. Epic and ballad, consequently, are not usually personal in point of view; self-expression is replaced by relating the deeds of others. Story-telling in verse, in either epic or ballad, probably arose from reciting myths during various rituals. The gods of myths were gradually replaced by kings and mortal heroes, resulting in what has come to be referred to as *heroic poetry* in which certain ideals of courage and honor are upheld by the hero of the story, who usually fights for some just cause (such as the regaining of a kingdom which has wrongly been taken from him). Epics like the *Iliad* and *Beowulf* derive much of their dramatic power from the lively narration of the hero's exciting deeds. Eventually English narrative poetry was freed from the narrative tradition, which required the telling of stories of great heroes and kings, and instead simply began to concentrate on stories of all kinds, such as Coleridge's long narrative poem, *The Rime of the Ancient Mariner* (as well as his wonderful, unfinished, mysterious "Christabel"). The Romantic poets, in fact, were extremely fond of story-telling in verse (we might think of Wordsworth's "Michael" or Keats' "The Eve of St. Agnes"). In the Victorian period Tennyson advanced the idea of narrative poetry by telling tales in poetry of Arthur and his knights of the Round Table, while Lord Macaulay drew his stories from ancient Rome.

In more recent times there has been less interest in narrative poetry, although there have been a few interesting experiments such as Rudyard Kipling's ballads and Stephen Vincent Benet's lengthy *John Brown's Body* (1928). Behind story-telling in verse as an art form is the rich epic tradition of the Italian Renaissance, as well as the numerous metrical tales written in the Middle Ages.

A Few Nongeneric Conventions

There are some conventions which do not "fit into" particular genres. These conventions are simply rules or agreements between poet and reader which are not at all dependent on the formal nature of the poem. These conventions, those which are not bound up with specific genres of poetry, are generally referred to as *motifs*, or recurring devices and themes. A few of the important ones follow.

CARPE DIEM. This is one of the most widely recurring motifs in English poetry. *Carpe diem** (Latin for "seize the day") poems are those in which the poet, to win over a beautiful lady, uses the argument that life must be enjoyed to the fullest now, in the present, because we do not know what the future will bring. *Carpe diem* poems are often humorous and witty. They generally make reference to the brevity of our time in this world, the inevitability of our dying, and the sheer fun of loving and being loved while in one's prime. Furthermore, it is hoped that the intellectual effort of argument will be immediately replaced by impulsive, spontaneous, sensual pleasure.

A good example of the *carpe diem* motif is found in Andrew Marvell's "To His Coy Mistress," the last part of which follows:

> Now, therefore, while the youthful hue
> Sits on thy skin like morning dew,
> And while thy willing soul transpires
> At every pore with instant fires,

* The phrase is from Horace, *Odes* I.11.

Now let us sport us while we may;
And now, like amorous birds of prey,
Rather at once our Time devour,
Than languish in his slow-chapt power.
Let us roll all our strength and all
Our sweetness up into one ball,
And tear our pleasures with rough strife
Through the iron gates of life.
Thus, though we cannot make our sun
Stand still, yet we will make him run.

In the following *carpe diem* motif poem, Shakespeare asks his lady to kiss him now while they are both young, for time will soon be spent:

O Mistress mine, where are you roaming?
O stay and hear! your true-love's coming
  That can sing both high and low;
Trip no further, pretty sweeting,
Journeys end in lovers' meeting—
  Every wise man's son doth know.
What is love? 'tis not hereafter;
Present mirth hath present laughter;
  What's to come is still unsure:
In delay there lies no plenty,—
Then come kiss me, Sweet-and-twenty,
  Youth's a stuff will not endure.

It should be noted, finally, that the *carpe diem* motif is not exclusively an instrument of *love* poetry. Sometimes it is used in Christian poems, which warn the reader about the inevitability of death and remind him of the attendant pleasures of the eternal life which will follow this temporal one (and the importance, therefore, of living righteously now).

Ubi Sunt Motif. *Ubi sunt* (Latin for "where are they?") poems are those in which poets wonder where time or youth have gone. This motif was extremely popular in medieval Latin poetry and has been tried with interesting results by numerous English poets. The question usually turns into a statement of the loss felt since time or an age has passed. The motif, then, is expressly nostalgic and tends to idealize what is irrecoverably past. The "where are they" question is of course rhetorical, for the poet and reader know exactly where they are—gone, vanished, *finis*.

DREAM-ALLEGORY. Another motif which is not dependent on the genre in which it is employed is the dream-allegory, a poem in which a poet (speaker) lies down, falls asleep in a beautiful garden or forest, and has a dream in which either real people or personified (allegorical) abstractions perform certain meaningful acts. This motif was most widely used during the Middle Ages and is perhaps best represented by Langland's *Piers Plowman*. The dream-allegory, sometimes called the dream vision, is an effective device for contrasting a dream state with a waking state, or for making apparent to a speaker a sense of reality which, ironically, he might not derive from reality itself. That is, upon waking, the poet-dreamer is usually aware of the great significance of what he has dreamed; thus the motif is frequently given a didactic orientation.

COURTLY LOVE CONVENTIONS. The medieval preference for dream-allegory was accompanied by a respect for the conventions of *courtly love*, a body of rules which many poets used when writing amatory verse. Courtly love is noble and idealized. A man in love treats his lady with great respect; however, it is one of the rules that this lady cannot be his wife. He wants to make love to her not simply to satisfy physical appetites, but also to achieve a beautiful moral existence. The irony of courtly love is that most of the poems dealing with it involve adultery, even though the adultery is entered into in the name of a search for truth, beauty, and perfection. Courtly love, this great love between a man and a woman who is not his wife, was made popular by Italian and French troubadors and then, through Petrarch, came to influence English poets, particularly Chaucer and Spenser (Chaucer used the conventions of courtly love a great deal, specifically in *Troilus and Cressida*, and Chaucer was Spenser's favorite poet). Courtly love became altered now and then as it was gradually absorbed by different poetic cultures. In general, though, the woman was always placed "higher" than the man who loved her; love itself was viewed as increasingly insatiable; human love, in its most basic sense, was considered an enriching, perfecting force.

PETRARCHAN LOVE. Petrarch carried forward and magnified that aspect of courtly love which focuses on the love-sick young man's bereaved, fearful condition. The *Petrarchan lover*—modeled after Petrarch himself who was frustrated in his great love for Laura, to whom he wrote his sonnet cycle—is conventionally love-sick, sad, and plaintive; he laments the hard-heartedness, coldness, and general lack of attention from his beloved. In expressing his enormous, unsatisfied love for a woman, the Petrarchan lover often uses antithesis and oxymoron (he follows her who causes all his pain), puns, and hyperbolic descriptions of the lady's charms. The Petrarchan love convention, then, is the juxtaposition of a lover who is unsatisfied in his great love for a beautiful woman, who, in turn, is apt to ignore his fervent advances. The Petrarchan lover generally feels resigned to failure in his love, and his resultant sadness provides the primary emotional mainspring of the motif. The poet, characteristically, hopes that his poem, written to his lady, will improve his situation. He hopes, as Sidney writes in the opening of his Petrarchan sonnet cycle, *Astrophel and Stella*, "That she, dear she, might take some pleasure of my pain." He writes because he is in pain at not having his great love reciprocated, but he nevertheless hopes that in writing down his thoughts he may be able to entertain—and thus favorably influence—the woman he loves. In the following sonnet, Samuel Daniel (1562–1619) assumes the role of a Petrarchan lover; he begins with an immediate coupling of his beloved's beauty and cruelty, and then continues to be plaintive:

FAIR IS MY LOVE

Fair is my Love, and cruel as she's fair;
Her brow-shades frown, although her eyes are sunny.
Her smiles are lightning, though her pride despair,
And her disdains are gall, her favours honey:
A modest maid, deck'd with a blush of honour,
Whose feet do tread green paths of youth and love;

The wonder of all eyes that look upon her,
Sacred on earth, deign'd a Saint above.
Chastity and Beauty, which were deadly foes,
Live reconciled friends within her brow;
And had she Pity to conjoin with those,
Then who had heard the plaints I utter now?
For had she not been fair, and thus unkind,
My Muse had slept, and none had known my mind.

Breaking with Convention

It should be pointed out that poets do not always make use of genres and their conventions, or of nongeneric conventions, in a pure way. While a poet who chooses a genre is limited by his choice (and, as we have mentioned, is also liberated from the trouble of having to explain all that he does), he nevertheless is ultimately free to make innovations within the tradition. He can modify certain conventions or he may simply omit some of them altogether. In general, he may alter any genre or convention to make it more meaningful in terms of his particular purpose as an artist.

Once a poet has chosen to write in a particular genre, he is committed to stay within certain broad limits, but he is perfectly free to modify some, but not all, of the conventions. Occasionally a poet *breaks with* an entire set of conventions; he is *substituting* a new set of conventions for the old set. Other poets will then need to decide whether to accept or reject these "new" conventions. *Breaking with conventions* can constitute either a good thing or a bad thing, depending on (1) whether a convention is broken intentionally or simply through carelessness and (2) whether, if intentionally, the reasons for the "breaking" seem consistent with what the poet is trying to do.

A good example of breaking with convention is provided by Wordsworth's decision to depart from the self-consciously "poetic" diction (a stylistic convention of the eighteenth century). Wordsworth was anxious to replace formal poetic diction with the natural speech of common people. Wordsworth's breaking with convention, in other words, was intentional and for the express purpose of purifying poetry into a language nearer to the real language of men (something more or less attempted in this century by Robert Frost). When Gerard Manley Hopkins substituted a system of stress for a system of regular poetic feet, producing what has come to be called *sprung rhythm*, he was breaking with the rules of regular stress for the explicit purpose of creating another kind of stress pattern. He was, therefore, trying to establish a new kind of relationship between meaning and meter. Breaking with convention more often than not has favorable results in that it stimulates new and different kinds of poetic activity. Thus the student should bear in mind that all of the genres which we have examined are, finally, open to the kind of creative ramifications which together form the exciting evaluation of poetry.

PART TWO

Drama

What Is Drama?

Northrop Frye has pointed out that the basic division of drama into tragedies and comedies is based on *verbal* drama, and therefore excludes such dramatic types as opera and masque. Within the verbal tradition, however, with which we are generally concerned in introductory college drama courses, a drama may be defined technically as a composition—written in prose, verse, or a combination of both—which presents a story in dialogue intended to be spoken on a stage. While "drama" designates what is meant to be given stage presentation, "dramatic art" designates plays from their writing to their actual production. Because there are many ingredients in a play—story, characters, action, language, imagery—no two plays are alike, and the college student writing about drama has as his constant task the recording of the *uniqueness* of the play under consideration.

While virtually every play is a *comedy* or a *tragedy* (or a *tragicomedy* or a *melodrama*), and thus has a certain amount in common with other plays, it usually has a significant independent existence. Every play has a particular *theme* (theme is a tricky word in dramatic criticism, but in its general acceptation means "subject" or "topic").

We have used the term "story" twice, first in our opening definition, and then in mentioning some of the ingredients of a drama. While every play has a story, we are generally inclined to discuss it in terms of *plot*. Aristotle, in a now famous definition, described plot as the soul of tragedy. Plot refers not simply to *what* happens in a play, but also to the *order* in which things happen, to the *sequence of events*.

Some critics, dwindling in number and perhaps in influence, assert that a play is not a play until it is performed; nevertheless, the *written text* of a play is still vital and still has a dramatic identity which we can define, describe, explain, and amplify. While a college student writing about drama is generally working with a written text, he should nevertheless try to imagine how certain events, conflicts, and speeches might appear on the stage. Drama, in the main, is an oral art, and the student must try to be sensitive to the sounds of a play and aware of the differences, for example, between quiet "asides" and thunderous commands. A dramatist thinks primarily in terms of a "live audience," and we, as *readers*, must try to keep that audience in mind. The play on the stage *is* more alive than it is in its written text, but with our *imagination*, we can feel the life which a play might have when staged. When a play is performed, the speeches are "blocked" or made to coincide with specific movements of the characters. The reader must try to picture in his mind the "live theatre" process of making physical movement a complement of speech.

Finally, a play is an *experience*. When we read a play we enter a world with a very particular identity. We attempt to describe that world, with all its *meaning*, by living inside of it for the duration of the play. Different kinds of plays, of course, produce different experiences, and this will become clear in our considerations of genre. But let us now turn to a consideration of some of the things which happen in *most* plays, to what, in other words, we generally are concerned with when we think about dramatic activity.

What Does Drama Do, and What Makes Drama Art?

It should be remembered at the outset that a play *entertains* an audience. A play is also a medium through which a dramatist "says" something to an audience on the other side. People go to the theatre for different reasons, of course, but none go to be bored. Whether or not they want to be made to erupt in belly-shaking laughter by a ribald farce or to be intellectually stimulated by the grim or ironic events of an antiwar play, they all want to be entertained. That is, their definitions of what is entertaining differ, but their desire to be entertained is uniform.

Naturally, what a play does depends to some extent on the specific kind of play it is. Sophocles' *Oedipus Rex* and Pirandello's *Six Characters in Search of an Author* obviously differ in the things they are doing. Nevertheless, there are certain things which these plays, and all plays, have in common.

Recalling our broad definition of art in our discussion of poetry—namely, that art is a craft which uses certain principles and methods and creates a product which is subject to aesthetic criteria—we turn now to the nature of dramatic art. As with our approach to poetry, our approach to drama may take three different courses. First, we must familiarize ourselves with certain specific principles of structure and characterization and established *dramatic techniques* or *methods* available to the dramatist as he creates his play. Secondly, there are certain dramatic *conventions*, just as we saw that there were certain poetic conventions. And finally, we need to understand and appreciate the ways in which a particular dramatist modifies, or "breaks with" conventions. How much freedom does a dramatist have? How logical does the plot of a play have to be? Must the hero die in order for the play to be a tragedy? In other words, as we examine dramatic principles, techniques, and conventions, we must try to be sensitive to the liberties which dramatists may take with them. As in poetry, so in drama we may discover considerable expressive variation on many "standard" dramatic principles and methods. This will be particularly important when we consider new developments in drama in the late nineteenth and early twentieth centuries (Shaw, Ibsen, Chekhov, Strindberg, Yeats) and in more recent experimental drama (Brecht, Pirandello, Stoppard). Because the *techniques* of structure and characterization are so essential to our discussion of them, we will combine our treatment of the "what" and the "how," and then move to a few other dramatic techniques which can be discussed separately as artistic devices.

Structure

GENERAL PRINCIPLES. For a play to do something, it has to make something, and what it makes is a *plot,* a series of events which together constitute dramatic *action.* As we have already noted, Aristotle defined plot as the first principle and soul of tragedy. Plot describes *what is,* or *what happens when.* The real importance of *structure* is that it suggests that certain things happen at certain times for particular, discernible reasons. The student writing about a play, therefore, should first make sure that he knows the exact order in which things happen and then attempt to explain the apparent artistic rationale behind that order. A certain amount of synthesis should take place: aspects of the plot must be related; logical connections between one part and another must be explained; the play, finally, must be seen as a unified, "organic whole." Characters' motives frequently link different parts of the plot; something which happens to a character in one place makes him do something in another.

The action of many plays, and particularly that of tragedies, forms a definite pattern. The conventional division of a tragedy suggests that the play has five parts: (1) *introduction*; (2) *rising action*; (3) *climax*; (4) *falling action*; and (5) a *catastrophe.* This plan, excepting catastrophe, is also common to most nontragic plays. In the *introduction* the audience meets some of the characters, becomes sensitive to the setting and situation, and begins to see anguish or humor around the corner. In the *rising action* a series of events occurs and this series results in some kind of *climax,* or main turning point. Often there is what we call the *exciting action,* usually an event which sets something in motion, an act which *excites* toward a particular change of events. Following the climax, there are further events which usually lead to the *catastrophe.* The *falling action* which comes *between* climax and *catastrophe* generally moves very swiftly. This overall pattern allows the audience to participate in the important *building* toward the final action. We will have more to say about this when discussing tragedy.

Expressed differently, all plays have some kind of *beginning, middle* and *end.* We need to be introduced to the *world* of the play and to be sensitive to a particular dramatic situation. Once introduced, something has to *happen,* and what happens must lead to a final result. In a comedy, events often lead to marriage, while in a tragedy, events lead to death. In both, events build upon one another in a particular fashion until a climax, or turning point, arrives. This climax then leads to the *resolution* of the particular problem with which the main characters are concerned.

Drama, like poetry, has immense flexibility of structure. A dramatist can spend as much time as he chooses in developing different sections of his play. Sometimes, for example, there is a very long introduction because the dramatist wants us to take our time in "getting the feel" of the play's world and characters. This occurs, for example, in Eugene O'Neill's long play *The Iceman Cometh.* In some plays, conflict is introduced early (A. C. Bradley has noticed that this is often true of Shakespeare's tragedies), while in other plays the conflict is introduced relatively late. *Othello* is not typical of Shakespeare, because the central conflict—Othello's enormous jealousy—is not brought into the play until the middle. That is, there is a long introduction, then swift rising action, climax (when Othello sees the supposed "proof" of Desdemona's guilt, her handkerchief), and a very rapid progression from climax to catastrophe (Othello's murder first of Desdemona and then of himself).

Every playwright, in short, expresses the personality of his drama through structure. We will have more to say about this when discussing *artistic structure*. Exposition, conflict, resolution; beginning, middle, end; introduction, rising action, climax, falling action, catastrophe—we are more or less concerned with the same kind of progression. The figure of a pyramid is often used to analyze dramatic structure. Through a series of crises the characters' various actions rise until, at the apex, some climax occurs which tends to "clear the air," and the characters proceed down the *other* side of the pyramid. This reducing of tension is generally known as *denouement*. In any case, every play contains some sort of movement which can be seen as roughly pyramidal; every play also contains *exposition*, that is, some relating of facts about past action (see *antecedent action*, p. 89).

In addition to perceiving the significance of *juxtapositions of scenes*, the student should be able to determine what any *one* particular scene contributes to the play (and plot) as a whole. I recently observed an English class, for example, in which the teacher assigned each student a different scene in *Macbeth* and asked him to explicate it (to make it plain or clear, to explain it, to interpret it) in terms of the *entire* play. Ideally, every scene has a discernible *function*, and thus we can usually determine whether a scene is "successful" or not. In most drama which is of processional structure—for example, Shakespeare's history plays—each scene leads to the next scene in an advancing manner, leading toward some *discovery*. Thus a scene is often said to *advance the plot*, meaning that a scene, in some specific way, brings the audience closer to the solution of some problem—for instance, closer to the discovery of a misunderstood identity (Viola in *Twelfth Night*) or toward the solving of a mysterious riddle (*Oedipus Rex*). Some plays, particularly so-called "discussion plays," are almost self-consciously disorganized and do not progress toward a fixed goal or climactic discovery. But even scenes in these plays contribute to the whole in particular ways. Each scene is meaningfully juxtaposed to another. The flexibility of dramatic structure is such that a dramatist can intentionally "break up" the order (that is, the *natural order*) of events so that dramatic interest is heightened. While we may think generally in terms of a pyramid, we must be sensitive to the ways in which a dramatist uses *each* scene; it may or may not fit neatly into the rising and falling pattern, but it probably makes a significant contribution to the overall scheme and introduces or deepens a dramatic quality of one kind or another.

Artistic Structure. In creating a play, a dramatist puts things together in a particular order for particular reasons. He is an individual artist whose product will be different, though sometimes only subtlely, from that of every other artist, and our constant concern is to suggest the artistry (and artistic implications) of the way in which a play is put together. We have already mentioned, for example, the conventional structure of much drama and most tragedy: introduction, rising action, climax, falling action, and catastrophe. *Dramatic technique* is discernible in the amount of time which each of these five sections of the play is given. A dramatist may spend as little or as much time as he wants in developing any one section of his play. It is very seldom that we find a five-act play which allows one act each for exposition, rising action, climax, falling action, and catastrophe. The climax is often delayed, for example, until late in the fourth act or early in the fifth act. While the catastrophe of a tragedy is generally a death which the audience has been expecting for some time, that death may come just before the curtain falls or it may come much earlier—though in general most dramatists consider it artistically weak to spend too much time "tying up loose ends" following the final death (see *denouement,* p. 84). When Hamlet says "The rest is silence" (V.ii.369), he more or less is reflecting the audience's expectation too—and, indeed, the play ends forty-five lines later.

Let us think further about the openings of plays. There are various ways of opening plays artistically, and a dramatist must choose among them. Sometimes, for example, a play opens with a speech by a major character—the Duke, Orsino, in *Twelfth Night* being discovered in his room saying, "If music be the food of love, play on"; Troilus in *Troilus and Cressida* asking, "Why should I war without the walls of Troy,/That find such cruel battle here within?" Sometimes, in contrast, a play opens with eerie, foreboding activity—the three officers, Bernardo, Francisco, and Marcellus, in *Hamlet* waiting for the mysterious apparition to come again, or the three witches cackling gleefully in the thunder and lightning as the curtain rises in *Macbeth*. The techniques of opening a play might be summarized as follows: (1) speech by a major character; (2) chit-chat of some minor characters; (3) a speech by the *chorus* (a group of speakers external to the action and thus able to comment on it with objectivity); (4) a *prologue*, in which a speaker appears and introduces the story to the audience (though the speech of a chorus and a prologue are really *pre*opening *devices*, for the real play, or play proper, only begins when some of the *characters* within the actual world of the drama begin to act and talk); and, of course, (5) an exchange of dialogue between major characters (though not necessarily including the hero—as, for example, the dialogue between Iago and Roderigo in the opening of *Othello*).

What the dramatist tries to do in the opening of his play is, logically, to *involve* the audience as quickly as possible. Sometimes this can be accomplished through effective animation of a particular environment or atmosphere—the storm scene, for example, which opens *The Tempest*. Sometimes the dramatist has a lowly character—or group of lowly characters—open the play by defining the central problem. We start *in media res** ("in the midst of things") and are swept up quickly into the play's world. This can be seen in the crisp, thematic opening of *Coriolanus*: a company of mutinous citizens with staves, clubs, and weapons enter onto the stage, and their dialogue proceeds as follows:

> 1. CIT. Before we proceed any further, hear me speak.
> ALL. Speak, speak.
> 1. CIT. You are all resolved rather to die than famish?
> ALL. Resolved, resolved.
> 1. CIT. First, you know Caius Marcius is chief enemy to all the people.
> ALL. We know't, we know't.
> 1. CIT. Let us kill him, and we'll have corn at our own price. Is't a verdict?

* This phrase, from Horace's *Ars Poetica* (148–150), refers primarily to epic, but is now also used in discussing other genres.

ALL. No more talking on't. Let it be done—away, away!
2. CIT. One word, good citizens.
1. CIT. We are accounted poor citizens, the patricians good. What authority surfeits on would relieve us. If they would yield us but the superfluity while it were wholesome, we might guess they relieved us humanely, but they think we are too dear. The leaness that afflicts us, the object of our misery, is an inventory to particularize their abundance, our sufferance is a gain to them. Let us revenge this with our pikes, ere we become rakes. For the gods know I speak this in hunger for bread, not in thirst for revenge.
2. CIT. Would you proceed especially against Caius Marcius?
ALL. Against him first. He's a very dog to the commonalty.
2. CIT. Consider you what services he has done for his country?
1. CIT. Very well, and could be content to give him good report for 't but that he pays himself with being proud.
2. CIT. Nay, but speak not maliciously.
1. CIT. I say unto you, what he hath done famously, he did it to that end. Though soft-conscienced men can be content to say it was for his country, he did it to please his mother and to be partly proud, which he is, even to the altitude of his virtue.

(I.i.1–41)

In this opening Shakespeare exerts great artistic control. He allows the audience to enter into the crowd of ordinary citizens protesting against what they consider their unjust treatment by the nobles and particularly by Caius Marcius (who is later given the name Coriolanus). Furthermore, the large problems with which the play will deal are all introduced. We have the grim, hostile polarization of the common people against the nobility; we also have dissent (through the first and second citizens) among the common people themselves; we have the beginnings of a pattern of famine imagery which will be sustained throughout the play; we have the all-important question raised as to the essential nature of Coriolanus' personality (namely, is he too *proud*, or is he simply a *sincere patriot*? His mother, who will play a large part in the play, is mentioned as the motivating force behind his deeds). The opening suggests vividly the nature of a very real and historically specific Roman world with its corn famine and bitter, starving people. Shakespeare read his historical source (Plutarch's *Lives*) carefully, and consequently this opening scene has a dramatic authenticity. Whenever a student begins to consider the craftsmanship of dramatic composition, he will usually find that the *nature of the opening* is significant. The dramatist can open his play in any number of ways, and the student should try to see why, *in terms of artistic choice*, it has in fact been opened in one particular way.

Most of what has been said about the openings of plays can be extended to the *artistic* possibilities for overall structural variation. Just as Shakespeare can decide to open *Coriolanus* with a debate among starving citizens, so too he can decide how, and at what rate of acceleration, the conflict between these citizens and Coriolanus will develop, at what point the antagonist (Aufidius) will be introduced, at what point Coriolanus will die, and how swiftly the play should end thereafter. (Actually, in this case, Shakespeare ends his play abruptly—twenty lines after the group of conspirators has murdered Coriolanus.)

In addition to thinking about a dramatist's creative experimentation with the structural components of his play, we should also think about internal action and "mentalistic" progress. Sometimes a play builds toward a climax primarily in terms of one character's mental outlook—usually presented through sharp changes in his attitude toward his own existence. This is certainly true of Milton's *Samson Agonistes*. His play ("dramatic poem") is modeled on Greek tragedy and has an appropriate catastrophe, but it lacks, as Dr. Johnson pointed out, a specific division into beginning, middle, and end. Instead of having a formal action, the middle of the play is taken up by a series of temptations presented to Samson. While these temptations do not constitute dramatic action per se, and thus do not form a formal "middle," they do dramatize the change in Samson—which in turn is responsible for advancing the play (thus exhibiting a form of "mentalistic" progress).

A more recent play which shows a similar independence from *present* action is Arthur Miller's *Death of a Salesman*. The major character, Willy Loman, is artfully introduced through the exposition of his pride in his sons, his feelings of superiority over his neighbors, and his general optimism about the future. This information about Willy constitutes the "introduction" of the play, and, as it is extended in terms of Willy's personality, it also becomes the rising action. The climax is not an event directly interrupting this sequence, but rather a flashback in time. Instead of an orderly progression from problem to solution (as, say, we find in *Hamlet* or *Coriolanus*), we have a muddling of the normal time scheme, and the climax takes the form of Biff Loman's *earlier* discovery that his father (whom he caught in a compromising situation with a woman in a Boston hotel) was a lecherous and unfaithful husband. Biff's climactic discovery, which is only revealed to Miller's audience in the middle of the play, deepens Willy Loman's problems, increases his feelings of despair, and further diminishes his self-respect. Willy's gradual acceptance of his failure constitutes the falling action of the play, and his suicide is the final catastrophe. The point here is that a dramatist can alter the time scheme, can use "flashbacks" as Miller does in *The Death of a Salesman,* in order to position the conflict and its resolution in a totally *psychological* progression (which is only occasionally given external expression through *present stage action*). In other words, a dramatist is not only concerned with the possibilities inherent in the length of different structural units (rising action, etc.), but is also anxious *to make the structural units reflect psychological change.*

ANTECEDENT ACTION. A playwright often needs to communicate to his audience certain information about events which have occurred *before* the opening of his play. Sometimes, as we have noted in our general discussion of structure, the playwright presents this background information, or *antecedent action,* in the exposition or introduction of the play. Sometimes he uses flashback material, as in Miller's *Death of a Salesman.* There is also the direct reporting or relating, at various times, of past events and circumstances, as in *The Tempest.* Then, too, there is choric summation, such as that which occurs throughout T. S. Eliot's *Murder in the Cathedral.* For example, Eliot repeatedly has the chorus summarize the hardness and uncertainty of the last seven years (the amount of time the archbishop has been gone):

> Seven years we have lived quietly,
> Succeeding in avoiding notice,
> Living and partly living.
> There have been oppression and luxury,
> There have been poverty and licence,
> There has been minor injustice.
> Yet we have gone on living,
> Living and partly living.

The chorus continuously summarizes the past at various points in the play, in order to remind the audience of the circumstances preceding those which we actually discover *in* the play.

Sometimes a dramatist presents *antecedent action* in a *combination* of ways, as, for example, when Claudius' antecedent murder of Hamlet's father is introduced by the appearance of Hamlet's father's ghost, by remarks made by Claudius, and by Hamlet's own words. The audience realizes that the antecedent action loiters, like the specter of Hamlet's father, very near to the present action, and, indeed, is even responsible for present action. (Antecedent action often provides motivation for present deeds.)

DENOUEMENT. The French verb *denouer* means "to untie, to untangle," and *denouement* denotes the same process. More specifically, *denouement* describes that section of the play in which the dramatist tries to untangle the various "loose ends" which have been introduced by the climax. Denouement is part of dramatic structure, but because of its flexibility, it seems worthy of being introduced here as a distinct dramatic technique. The dramatist usually devotes a particular section of his play to the resolution of the plot; *denouement* refers both to this section of clarification and resolution, and also to the exact point at which this section begins. Some dramatists, particularly certain modern ones, omit denouement in order to leave the audience with a certain amount of intentional ambiguity or uncertainty. In this manner the dramatist allows his audience to do its own clarifying; he hopes that the events, taken together, will communicate his message in and by themselves. The way in which a dramatist untangles the plot, then, is a reflection of artistic decision-making. Perhaps a character will enter with a new piece of evidence which clears everything up. Perhaps a character will explain things in the act of dying. Sometimes we find the device of *deus ex machina*: a god (usually in a classical Greek play) resolves the play's entanglements by way of *supernatural intervention*. Many critics, understandably, deplore this device, because it is so patently a simplistic solution.

REVERSAL. Another important element of structural consideration is *reversal*, the dramatic "turning point" in the fortune of a play's hero. Reversal designates the exact point in the plot when the hero suddenly and necessarily shifts the course of action which he has, up until now, been following. When the reversal occurs, the hero is usually faced with the realization that the fate which awaits him is *not* the fate which he had expected. Usually he does something because he expects a certain result, but the deed instead leads to a different result. Aristotle has defined this change as *peripetia* (reversal). When Cleopatra has reported to Antony the news that she is dying, she hopes this news will make him come rushing to her. Instead, Antony kills himself. Juliet swallows a harmless potion to make it appear that she is dead, so that her body will be taken away and she can then be reunited with Romeo. But Romeo finds her in her swoon and, believing she is dead, kills himself. When she awakens and finds him dead, she kills herself. Thus her planned reunion with Romeo arrives, unexpectedly, through death. Cleopatra's plan and Juliet's plan (their respective *deeds*) bring about *reversed* results. Shakespeare uses reversal to determine plot, of course, but also to surprise his audience in a dramatic way. Reversal, like soliloquy, is a dramatic device used to heighten the audience's almost visceral, or instinctive, concern for what is happening in the play.

SUSPENSE. A dramatist generally tries to create suspense; that is, the audience is made to experience curiosity, uncertainty, and excitement, because it does not know the outcome. Suspense is a kind of stretching of the audience's anxiety. One structural technique of heightening suspense is to delay the climax until a relatively late point in the play. The audience's desire to know what is going to happen in the end is heightened, because the dramatist deliberately frustrates that desire. Sometimes suspense is created not through structural strategy, but through overwhelmingly interesting characters; the audience is able to identify with a particular character and begins to believe that his future is theirs. A dramatist also heightens suspense by hinting at—but not declaring—what is going to happen (this method is generally called *foreshadowing*); sometimes, too, irony heightens suspense, for while we have a fairly good idea of how the events are going to turn out, we enjoy watching a character, unaware of the meaning of various actions, discover for himself the nature of his fate. By all of these means, and often several of them together, a dramatist artistically tries to heighten our involvement in his dramatic world.

Characters

General Principles. All plays are composed of characters who, through their actions and dialogues, generate a dramatic whole. The substance of a play is larger than the sum of the substances of the characters, because additional information is transmitted through *character interaction.* A play introduces representatives of people from the real world. These people are *characterized* in the play through their own spoken words, through their deeds, and through the comments which other characters in the play make about them.

Some characters are more substantially involved in the main action of a play than others. Some, conversely, are more *external* to that action. Shakespeare's Macbeth is very much *involved;* Shakespeare's railer Jaques in *As You Like It* is not. Those characters who are substantially involved in the main action are *major characters;* those less involved are *minor characters.* While the major characters are usually the most complex, there are countless exciting minor characters. Indeed, some readers of Shakespeare's plays are more interested in his whole collection of fools, clowns, villains' assistants, prelates, and railers than they are in his great tragic figures like Lear and Macbeth.

After a dramatist has introduced characters (this of course must happen immediately), he begins to *deepen* them by increasing the complexity of their decisions, conflicts, motives, and relationships with one another. The nature of the conflict is of course bound up with the nature of the play, but the conflict must necessarily arise out of the interaction of the personalities of the different characters.

Resolution of problems generally depends on changes in at least some of the characters who are, after all, the ones the audience sees moving around on a stage. While many characters can be *typed* (*the* prodigal, *the* hero, *the* clown, etc.), they usually become more than types. Students should try, first, to be perceptive about characters and then try to discuss them in the most *meaningful* way possible. The dramatist may wish to have "*a* clown" in his play, but the result is not really "*a* clown" but rather a very particular clown created in a special way and for special purposes. The point does not need elaboration: the general naming of a character as "tragic" or "comic" does not satisfy us, because the reader needs to be told *how* and *to what extent* the character is tragic or comic; similarly, the *typing* of a character (hero, clown, etc.) does not satisfy us, because a reader wants to know about a *particular* character. Every play, then, depends on its characters, and yet becomes something greater than them. A play reflects its characters in the sense that if one character represents one abstract thing (sometimes called a "thematic character") and another character something else, and they clash, the play becomes a composition about that clash. The activity of the characters—located variously nearer to divine events or to human ones—generates the definition of the play's meaning. A dramatic genre becomes a composition about itself in the sense that certain characters are first presented and *then* proceed to let us know what kind of play they are *in*. Drama *is* an imitation of life, and life, as most of us experience it, does produce conflict. Drama mirrors, through the behavior and words of its characters, the conflict which in various ways lies at the center of all human activity.

A student is often asked to write an analysis of the characters of a play. There are several ways of doing this. It is important to be sure to describe characters factually, that is, to summarize what one knows about a particular character as the play begins and what is added to that knowledge by the opening scenes of the play. Shakespeare's Othello is "a Moor," as he was in Shakespeare's source (Cinthio's *Hecatomithi*), but in that source "a

Moor" meant only a man converted to a Saracen on the northern coast of Africa. Shakespeare's Othello is quite definitely also a Negro, a black man, and the opening act of the play contains numerous references to his blackness, particularly in the remarks sputtered out by the enraged Brabantio. This sort of factual account of a character is important to any written analysis, particularly because the writer does not carelessly assume too much knowledge, perhaps lacking, on the part of his reader.

A student can usually write about the *motivation* of characters, that is, attempt to *explain* their *behavior* in psychological terms. Most playwrights have a good grasp on psychological concepts. Freud may have supplied names and labels for certain of our "hang-ups" (a post-Freudian phrase, of course), but Shakespeare and his contemporaries were completely familiar with them and utilized them in their characters.

In addition to description and explanation of motivation, the student usually needs to write about *changes* in characters during the course of the play or about *character development.* Most characters in plays are not *static,* but instead are generally perceived as *developing.* Jealousy may deepen (Othello), desire for revenge may increase and lead to a kind of madness (Hamlet), or guilt may lead to total depression and suicide (Lady Macbeth). A character changes as he becomes more involved in the events of the play. Basic human emotions (love, hate, greed, envy, respect, etc.) are not particularly stable and their instability provides the backdrop for what happens in a play. Some characters are developed more extensively than others, and, naturally, a dramatist spends most of his time developing his major characters. Nevertheless, there is often striking change in the behavior of some of the minor, subordinate characters. In any case, a student needs to understand what a character is like in the beginning of a play, what he is like in the end of the play, and what has happened to him in between.

A character, in other words, has an *ethically neutral physical identity,* a will which functions in an ethical manner and determines the degree of morality of his behavior, and also a *role.* A villain is given the *role* of evil-doer, and a hero the *role* of good-doer. Analysis of characters in a drama must take into account the precise nature of any given role, because a role leads to a certain amount of relatively conventional action. Certain kinds of plays, furthermore, inevitably contain certain roles. For example, a revenge tragedy like Thomas Kyd's *The Spanish Tragedy*, or *Hamlet*, must have an *avenger*. A so-called New Comedy, such as those written by Menander, must have a *senex* (an old man who meddles in the love affairs of the young). Every kind of play is a particular assembly of character roles, and while a dramatic character usually combines *identity, will* and *role*, the play in which he appears attempts to reflect real life. The three components of dramatic character are merged; physical traits like fatness or baldness combine with considerations of will, and moral decisions are often made in accord with the demands of role.

The three components of dramatic character, then, are always intertwined, though with varying depth and obscurity. Furthermore, a dramatist does not always point directly to the motivation behind a particular act. A play, in offering us real-life representatives, does not pretend that its characters are completely predictable or understandable, and many good playwrights deliberately leave many considerations of human nature ambiguous. At the end of *Troilus and Cressida*, the railing rogue Thersites is allowed to live, but not for any particular reason. Hector asks him if he is a good match for his might; Thersites replies that he is nothing but a railing knave; Hector says he believes him and thus will let him live. Is Hector's real motive clear? It is too late in the play to look for the answer by appealing to a social concept like honor, which has already been deeply attacked. Thersites' presence in the play has changed nothing. His will, such as it is, has not been completely understood, nor has the extremely melancholy nature of his identity. In other words, when *writing* about characters, one must always remember their *human complexity*. Indeed, character development in a play is exciting sometimes simply *because* we cannot answer enough questions.

The importance of *role* cannot be underestimated. A character in a play must be seen at all times not only as an individual, but as someone carrying out a conventional course of action (falling in love, revenging a father's murder, discovering an explanation for a mystery). Some kinds of behavior and speech are appropriate to a particular role and some are not. A young man in love may be blind to the implications of an act, but a king cannot afford to be blind. Finally, since certain kinds of plays require certain roles, the *way* in which a particular dramatist develops roles —the villain, the young girl in love—provides a good basis of comparison between his play and other plays. Characters must seem, in the light of their roles, to be *experiencing life plausibly*. That is, they must be *believable* to the audience. And, to a lesser extent perhaps (though this is a subtle distinction), so must their actions —which leads us to our next consideration.

ARTISTIC CHARACTERIZATION. When a dramatist attempts to make his characters "believable" he employs several techniques. The first, of course, is mention of their physical appearance. A character in a play usually looks like himself a little more than he might in real life; that is, his appearance is apt to be exaggerated. Richard III with his crooked back and black clothes *looks* like the villain he is. Falstaff with his enormous belly *looks* self-indulgent. Hamlet, usually dressed in black, is slender and aesthetic-looking. Willy Loman wears a worn suit, his hair is grayed, and his eyes are tired (who will forget his magnificent portrayal by Lee J. Cobb?). In other words, a dramatist must visualize his characters and carefully remind his audience of their physical identity.

Secondly, it perhaps goes without saying that the most characteristic thing about a man is the way he speaks. What kinds of words does he use? What sort of gestures accompany his speech? Does he raise or lower his voice, and if so, at what times? Does he speak with sweet reasonableness or with thundering passion? When we first meet the new king, Claudius, in *Hamlet*, we know that his words, and indeed his manner of speaking, are appropriately "kingly":

> Though yet of Hamlet our dear brother's death
> The memory be green, and that it us befitted
> To bear our hearts in grief and our whole kingdom
> To be contracted in one brow of woe,
> Yet so far hath discretion fought with nature

That we with wisest sorrow think on him,
Together with remembrance of ourselves.

(I.ii.1–7)

These words seem appropriate to the audience; they have a seriousness and dramatic stateliness which we consider logical in the speech of someone who is taking over as the head of state. The words also introduce us to a leader's natural psychology of optimism.

In contrast, consider the words and manner of speaking of Shylock in *The Merchant of Venice;* after meeting Antonio, Shylock forcefully utters an extended aside which lets us know that he is villainous:

How like a fawning publican he looks!
I hate him for he is a Christian,
But more for that in low simplicity
He lends out money gratis and brings down
The rate of usance here with us in Venice.
If I can catch him once upon the hip,
I will feed fat the ancient grudge I bear him.
He hates our sacred nation, and he rails,
Even there where merchants most do congregate,
On me, my bargains, and my well-worn thrift,
Which he calls interest. Cursed be my tribe
If I forgive him!

(I.iii.42–53)

The self-characterization of this speech is quite evident. All of Shylock's attitudes and personality traits are clear. It is as if he is simply stepping out, and saying to the audience, "let me tell you a little about myself." This happens frequently in Shakespeare's plays, but particularly with the characterization of villains. A good example is offered by the extended soliloquy of the villainous Richard in the opening of *Richard III*. Part of the soliloquy follows:

But I, that am not shaped for sportive tricks,
Nor made to court an amorous looking-glass;
I, that am rudely stamped, and want love's majesty
To strut before a wanton ambling nymph;

> I, that am curtailed of this fair proportion,
> Cheated of feature by dissembling nature,
> Deformed, unfinished, sent before my time
> Into this breathing world, scarce half made up,
> And that so lamely and unfashionable
> That dogs bark at me as I halt by them—
> Why, I, in this weak piping time of peace,
> Have no delight to pass away the time,
> Unless to spy my shadow in the sun
> And descant on mine own deformity.
> And therefore, since I cannot prove a lover,
> To entertain these fair well-spoken days,
> I am determined to prove a villain
> And hate the idle pleasures of these days.
>
> (I.i.14–31)

Richard has called attention to his rude physical deformity, his unfitness for love, his "spoiler" personality, and his villainous *role* in the play. As one last example of dramatic self-characterization, consider these lines by Falstaff from *Henry IV* (Part I):

> Bardolph, am I not fallen away vilely since
> this last action? Do I not bate? Do I not dwindle?
> Why, my skin hangs about me like an old lady's
> loose gown, I am withered like an old applejohn.
>
> (III.iii.1–4)

With these ironic words Falstaff invites the audience to joke with him over his comic pretense to be thin and wizened like an old apple—when he is quite obviously very fat! This is a good example of self-characterization, because it reminds us that we do not always take *literally* the things characters say about themselves. Sometimes they fail to point out their most obvious features, and this is one of the dramatist's ways of using irony—the conspicuous omission of reference to traits makes them obvious.

Another method of communicating the nature of a character to the audience is through the character's *reactions* to events. He may be easily depressed or unusually stoic in the face of sudden adversity; he may be annoyed or delighted by being the brunt of some other character's joke. To talk about characters' reactions is, really, to talk about characters *in the action.* That is, the art of characterization depends on the dramatist's successful *manipulation* of character. What a character does in a certain situation is part of his nature. Hamlet is, of course, playing the conventional *role* of the avenger, but there must be a certain logic and emotional relevance about the way he, as an individual, reacts to events.

A play has no formal narration or description. There is only dialogue. Characters often talk about each other. These comments constitute an important part of characterization (though generally a dramatist relies more substantially on the art of self-characterization through speech and action than he does on commentary by other characters).

When writing about a play we generally try to evaluate the characterization in terms of *believability.* Does it seem *possible* and, further, *probable* that a character acts the way he does? Is the personality of the character consistent, or does he act in ways which seem illogical or overtly antithetical? Does the character have any depth, or is he simply a "type"? Our general feeling is that the "best" characters in drama are those who achieve a definite reality, those who seem, given what we know of human nature, to be honest possibilities. A dramatist's *art* of characterization is successful to the extent that the audience accepts the major characters (and, hopefully, some of the minor ones) as *people* (not simply as particular *roles*). Hamlet is an avenger and is a good example of that role, but he is also a very poignant, melancholy, and disturbed young *man.* Shakespeare's character is exciting, because both the real person and the role are suggested. Ideally, a dramatist shows us the essential humanity of his world, for he knows that no audience is satisfied with wooden, mechanical puppets.

SOLILOQUY. A soliloquy is the act of talking while alone (or even *as if* alone). We need to add "as if," because sometimes a person is disregardful of, or oblivious to, the presence of any possible "listeners." The soliloquy is one of the most conventional *devices* of drama. It allows the playwright to present the character's deepest, innermost thoughts—which, given the final privacy of human nature, it would be illogical for him to share with others. As a device in drama the soliloquy is a perfect vehicle through which the dramatist may use his finest, most expressive language. Because the soliloquy is such a conventional device, however, it sometimes becomes too mechanical in its deliberate, self-conscious laying bare of a character's soul. Sometimes, in other words, the typicality of the device seems to detract from its sincerity. Nevertheless, some of the most expressive language of drama is discovered in soliloquies. Certainly few dramatic utterances surpass the masterful language of Shakespeare's soliloquies. We can consider the opening of Hamlet's well-known soliloquy:

> Oh, that this too too solid flesh would melt,
> Thaw, and resolve itself into a dew!
> Or that the everlasting had not fixed
> His canon 'gainst self-slaughter! Oh, God! God!
> How weary, stale, flat, and unprofitable
> Seem to me all the uses of this world!
> Fie on't, ah, fie! 'Tis an unweeded garden
> That grows to seed, things rank and gross in nature
> Possess it merely. That it should come to this!
> But two months dead! Nay, not so much, not two.
> So excellent a king, that was, to this,
> Hyperion to a satyr. So loving to my mother
> That he might not beteem the winds of heaven
> Visit her face too roughly.
>
> (I.ii.129–142)

Hamlet's personalized, innermost feelings are carefully self-expressed. The audience feels that he is a *real person*, a painfully unhappy young man, and not simply the avenger *role* in the play. Soliloquies, as dramatic devices, afford opportunities for *deepening* characters and thus for increasing the audience's involvement in the play.

Gesture and Language

Gesture refers to the physical movements (of all sizes) of characters on the stage: entering, exiting, embracing, swinging limbs, falling down, standing up, making pointed facial expressions. All verbal drama is based on dialogue, but the reader must be sensitive to the juncture of speech *and* movement, to physical and verbal coordination. Sometimes the exit of a character, or the single flopping of the hand from a character's wrist, *says* more than any accompanying verbal statement.

Gesture is an important part of the broad "language" of a play, though not of its rhetoric. The speeches contain all of the rhetoric, and the flavor of the colloquial diction of the time which the dramatic world reflects. Every play depends on language (thinking, still, of verbal drama); language provides the essential medium through which characters communicate, and it also establishes, with considerable *precision,* the nature of the problems implicit in the characters' actions. For example, sometimes the audience understands what is happening to a character without being *told.* The dramatist knows this; he uses language as a way of deepening characterization or of providing the rhetorical pattern implied by the events. Consider, for example, the way in which a brief bit of dialogue defines the forthcoming experience of Faustus near the opening of Act II of Marlowe's play:

> FAUSTUS. First will I question thee about hell.
> Tell me, where is the place that men call hell?
> MEPHISTOPHELES. Under the heavens.
> FAUSTUS. Aye, but whereabout?
> MEPHISTOPHELES. Within the bowels of these elements,
> Where we are tortured and remain forever.
> Hell hath no limits, nor is circumscribed
> In one self place, for where we are is hell,
> And where hell is there must we ever be;
> And, to be short, when all the world dissolves
> And every creature shall be purified,
> All places shall be hell that is not heaven.
> FAUSTUS. I think hell's a fable.
> MEPHISTOPHELES. Aye, think so, till experience change thy mind.
> (II.i.116–127)

While this is dialogue, verbal communication between two principal characters in the play, it is also rhetoric, incisive amplification of the nature of Faustus' coming quest and a comment on the meaning of his forthcoming fate. During the course of the play Faustus learns the nature of hell; this dialogue helps the audience keep that learning in its proper perspective. It also happens that Marlowe is using *blank verse* (unrhyming lines of iambic pentameter) which makes the language rhythmical and poetic. The point is that every dramatist uses language in different ways, with varying changes in the proportions of formal speech and colloquial speech (if indeed he uses *both*), and language, in the broad sense of speech *and* gesture, serves as an excellent basis for comparison between one play and another.

All plays do some of the same things with language. For example, language permits self-characterization (to the extent that a person's diction and way of speaking reflects his personality), provides rhetoric for boundaries of problems, differentiates characters in terms of class distinctions (in *A Midsummer Night's Dream*, for example, we have the stately language of the members of the court, the more human, romantic language of the young lovers, the "low" or rough language of Bottom and his actors, etc.), provides high points in the verbal expression of the action (the *soliloquies*, for example, of tragic heroes, or the cynical speeches of realists like Shakespeare's Jaques or Mercutio), defines and organizes for the audience the nature of the conflict, foreshadows or suggests what is to come, and—let us not underestimate the importance of this—comments on the action.

There are many other common uses of language in drama. Even nonverbal drama in its reliance on mime and gesture is dependent on speech, because it conspicuously omits it! Finally, it should be remembered that plays derive great force and contrast from varying the *volume* of the verbal expression—the quietly uttered aside, the subdued soliloquy, the bantering argument, the noisy battling, and the sweet or cheeky *singing*, respectively, of heroines and clowns. Variations in volume, in diction, and in rhetorical content provide the outlines for character development and the basis for generating dramatic *qualities*, if not always dramatic action.

Situation

Before writing about a play one must be certain to have in mind its logical, physical, and chronological circumstances, that is, its *situation.* The situation of a play is *more* than simple setting—which suggests *only* the physical location and its characteristics—but *less* than the entire action. The situation includes the setting, the prevailing atmosphere, and, often, the general state of mind of the characters. The situation of a play, in other words, is its overall makeup and often provides the genesis of the action. In the opening of Marlowe's *Dr. Faustus,* for example, part of the situation is Faustus' strong desire to become something more than a man, that is, his desire to surpass his earthly limits. This aspect of the situation provides the logic behind his decision to take the advice of Cornelius and Valdes to try magic, which in turn leads to the appearance of Mephistopheles and to everything else that follows. In order to understand the movement of a play one needs to be very sensitive to the entire situation of its opening.

Atmosphere, as an integral part of dramatic situation, refers to the *mood* or emotional framework of either a particular scene or the complete play: the mysterious, foreboding opening of *Hamlet,* the drawing-room gentility of *Le Misanthrope,* the bawdy tavern atmosphere of the cavorting of Prince Hal and Falstaff in the *Henry IV* plays, and so forth. Atmosphere is the dramatist's manner of depicting the *world* in which a particular group of characters exists.

When we move, within the course of a play, from one place to another, we use our imagination to allow the stage to be different places. We go back and forth from Alexandria to Rome, for example, in *Antony and Cleopatra,* making what Coleridge termed a "willing suspension of our disbelief." A play demands imaginative participation in every facet of the situation. We must be *sensitive* to the setting, place, and atmosphere and *perceptive* about the feelings of the various characters.

Dramatic landscapes become larger, or more significant, than their physical properties suggest, and if a student wishes to write meaningfully about a play, to provide the rhetoric of discussion of drama, he must first and most importantly be perceptive about overall "situation." There is simply no better place to begin, nor better point of entry into the dramatist's intention.

Affirmation

A play generally affirms—asserts—that something *is,* or *is true.* If a play affirms something which we probably already believe (accept), it is a play of *confirmation* or ratification. *Othello* affirms the evil nature of jealousy and confirms us in our fears of the consequences of jealousy. This is the most basic sense of the play. Naturally there are other meanings to discover. Because a play attempts to affirm something, the playwright may often be said to have certain *values.* He may endorse certain social concepts like freedom or honor; he may despise avarice, lechery, or war; he may feel that romantic love is futile. In any case, the playwright's values, the values which he inserts into the play through his characters and their actions, usually "add up" to some kind of affirmation. When writing about a play, then, a student is asked to consider meaning. Why do characters behave in certain ways? Why does the play end this way? The answers to these and similar questions provide us with sufficient material to determine precisely what the play affirms—a need to recognize that we all have "pipe-dreams" (illusions) in O'Neill's *The Iceman Cometh,* an awareness of the idea that the sins of the father are visited on his children in Ibsen's *Ghosts,* the sad consequences of family feuds in *Romeo and Juliet,* the futility of war in *Troilus and Cressida,* the tragic results of the clash of different social classes in Strindberg's *Miss Julie,* and so forth.

To say that a play *affirms* something about certain aspects of human activity is to say that a play is *not* simply "about" something. To identify a theme, or central topic (jealousy, love, war), is not, in itself, sufficient; rather, we need to know the exact nature of the dramatist's *attitude* toward that theme and how that attitude is demonstrated within the play. Presumably a playwright decides to write a play (or, as with Ionesco's *The Bald*

Soprano, an "antiplay") because he has strong feelings which he wants to present. The dramatist assigns value, worth, or merit to the characters of whom he approves and offers his personal appraisal of human behavior. It follows that the audience, by studying the nature of the characters and what becomes of them, can define quite clearly what is being *affirmed* in the play.

With these considerations of character, action, structure, situation, meaning, and language in mind, that is, with this familiarity with what all verbal drama does, let us now turn to a consideration of a few other dramatic techniques.

Other Dramatic Techniques

IMAGERY. Imagery functions in drama with a good deal of similarity to the ways in which it functions in poetry. An image is a description of something which attempts to set forth, through a comparison, the essence of that thing. An image, in other words, is a small picture, or a suggestion of the quality of something through an appropriate analogy. An image is intended to symbolize, represent, or suggest. Most images draw attention to a certain characteristic of something or someone by suggesting a parallel, analogical one. Images often have a certain moral content; light is often associated with the forces of right and goodness, while darkness is associated with the forces of wrong and evil. Murders are more apt to take place on dimly lit stages, while marriages and festivals are filled with bright light (the pattern of imagery of darkness and light is known by the Italian term as *chiaroscuro*).

While isolated images in a play may seem relatively unimportant, they form significant *patterns of imagery*. For example, there is the pattern of disease imagery in *Hamlet* which is evident even in the smallest ways; for example, when Claudius is reminding the audience of the disease-like nature of vicious gossip, Claudius worries about Laertes' return:

Poor Ophelia
Divided from herself and her fair judgment,

> Without the which we are pictures, or mere beasts.
> Last, and as much containing as all these,
> Her brother is in secret come from France,
> Feeds on his wonder, keeps himself in clouds,
> And wants not buzzers to infect his ear
> With pestilent speeches of his father's death.
>
> (IV.v.84–91)

The "buzzers," or scandalmongers, "infect" Laertes' ear, making "pestilent" remarks. These words relate Laertes' coming deeds to Hamlet's avenging nature which itself is also frequently seen as a pestilence or disease which "infects" his nature. What is even more important is that the image reflects the nature of the act by which Hamlet's father was murdered (poisoned in the ear); the whole play contains multiple references to poisoning and decay, all of which form a larger pattern of disease imagery.

Sometimes imagery is used to develop characters. That is, while disease imagery in *Hamlet,* or the imagery of magic in *Othello,* tends to have its basic suggestiveness in terms of the theme of the play, some images are a part of basic characterization and often replace some of the more "descriptive" functions of prose fiction. A good example of characterization through imagery is the constant figurative *picturing* of Iago as a spider planning to entrap a fly. We might also think of the way in which the villainous Richard III is steadily associated with a kind of poisonous toad. In *Henry IV* (Part I), there is a wonderful scene in the Eastcheap tavern in which the fat, rollicking Falstaff first plays Prince Hal's father, and then plays Hal. In this second case, the prince pretends to be his own father and speaks to Falstaff, playing Hal, about his worthless, fat companion Falstaff; the images of fatness and beastliness are used humorously here (as they are throughout the play) to help characterize Falstaff as a self-indulgent, overweight, drunken sensualist:

> PRINCE (*acting as his own father*). Swearest thou, ungracious boy? Hence forth ne'er look on me. Thou art violently carried away from grace. There is a devil haunts thee in the likeness of an old fat man, a tun of man is thy companion. Why dost thou converse with that trunck of humors, that bolting hutch

> of beastliness, that swollen parcel of dropsies, that huge bombard of sack, that stuffed cloack bag of guts, that roasted Manningtree ox with the pudding in his belly, that reverend vice, that gray iniquity, that father ruffian, that vanity in years? Wherein is he good, but to taste sack and drink it? Wherein neat and cleanly, but to carve a capon and eat it? Wherein cunning, but in craft? Wherein crafty, but in villainy? Wherein villainous, but in all things? Wherein worthy, but in nothing?
>
> (II.iv.490–505)

Falstaff, playing the young prince who must defend his fat friend to his father, cleverly replies by saying he wishes the king would explain himself, because he is not sure who is meant, and then he too carries forward the imagery of fatness and thinness. The dialogue proceeds from the last quoted speech in this manner:

> FALSTAFF. I would your grace would take me with you. Whom means your grace?
>
> PRINCE. That villainous, abominable misleader of youth, Falstaff, that old white-bearded Satan.
>
> FALSTAFF. My lord, the man I know.
>
> PRINCE. I know thou dost.
>
> FALSTAFF. But to say I know more harm in him than in myself were to say more than I know. That he is old, the more the pity, his white hairs do witness it; but that he is, saving your reverence, a whore-master, that I utterly deny. If sack and sugar be a fault, God help the wicked! If to be old and merry be a sin, then many an old host that I know is damned. If to be fat be to be hated, then Pharaoh's lean kine are to be loved. No, my good lord. Banish Peto, banish Bardolph, banish Poins. But for sweet Jack Falstaff, kind Jack Falstaff, true Jack Falstaff, valiant Jack Falstaff, and therefore more valiant, being, as he is, old Jack Falstaff, banish not him thy Harry's company. Banish plump Jack, and banish all the world.
>
> PRINCE. I do, I will.
>
> (II.iv.506–526)

The associations the audience makes with Falstaff's character are to the seven deadly sins (sloth, gluttony, etc.). He is pictured throughout the play in *animal images* which continuously suggest the animal nature of his person and habits. The dialogue we have just examined *reinforces* what is said about Falstaff in other places and amplifies the meaning of what *he* himself says to others during the course of the play. For example, at one point earlier in this same scene, Falstaff had deftly characterized Prince Hal by using images of thinness:

> FALSTAFF. 'Sblood, you starveling, you elf skin, you dried neat's tongue, you bull's pizzle, you stock-fish! Oh, for breath to utter what is like thee! You tailor's yard, you sheath, you bow case, you vile standing tuck——.
>
> PRINCE. Well, breathe a while, and then to it again, and when thou hast tired thyself in base comparisons, hear me speak but this.
>
> (II.iv.270–277)

Falstaff's "base comparisons" are typical of many of those made by all of the characters throughout the play; the comparisons are images which, taken collectively, bear on the play's meaning as well as on the identities of its contrasting characters. In this particular play images are used to exaggerate characterization; by repeatedly calling attention to Hal as skinny and to Falstaff as fat, Shakespeare makes Hal the young prince and Falstaff the old sensualist.

Images are used, then, to strengthen the theme and to aid in characterization. Images are also often used to dramatize concepts and to make things more visually present to the audience. Many images are used just once, though often one image is reinforced by another. In *Henry IV* (Part II) Warwick calls attention to the way in which Prince Hal is self-consciously spending time with Falstaff simply in order to learn about life; Warwick uses the following image:

> The prince but studies his companions
> Like a strange tongue, wherein, to gain the language,
> 'Tis needful that the most immodest word
> Be looked upon and learned, which once attained,
> Your highness knows, comes to no further use
> But to be known and hated. So, like gross terms,

> The Prince will in the perfectness of time
> Cast off his followers, and their memory
> Shall as a pattern or a measure live,
> By which his Grace must note the lives of others,
> Turning past evils to advantages.
>
> (IV.iv.68–78)

Warwick's image, comparing knowledge of human nature to knowledge of a language, is not repeated. It helps, at this moment in the play, to dramatize the nature of the young Hal's friendship with Falstaff. Another part of this image's dramatic power, however, is its relationship to similar images in the other *Henry IV* plays; for example, in *Henry V*, Ely is explaining that Prince Hal has changed, in his own private way, during the course of his companionship with Falstaff and others:

> ELY. The strawberry grows underneath the nettle,
> And wholesome berries thrive and ripen best
> Neighbored by fruit of baser quality.
> And so the prince obscured his contemplation
> Under the veil of wildness, which no doubt
> Grew like the summer grass, fastest by night,
> Unseen, yet crescive in his faculty.
>
> (I.i.60–66)

This last line means that the strawberry, representing Hal, has been growing by its own natural power while perhaps veiled amid the company of rascals like Falstaff. Thus, while it may at first appear that a particular image is singular or isolated, the student should study it carefully and try to discover whether the image is, in fact, making an analogy similar to the analogies of other images. Any formal criticism of a play must take account of its imagery. The main intention is to discover the primary pattern. The images combine to form what Northrop Frye has termed the play's "tonality," something similar to the system of tones or tints in a picture. This tonality is developed through the repetition of similar words on the audience's ear. The imagery of a play, like the tonality of a painting, is the sum of all the parts, and that is why a particular, unified pattern of imagery will have its dramatic effect.

Dramatic Irony. Irony occurs when words express a meaning which is opposite of the *intended* meaning. In drama, there are several kinds of irony. *Verbal irony* occurs when characters say things which *they* think mean one thing when, in fact, to the audience, they mean another; the words, when spoken ironically, tend to *indicate* attitudes which are opposite to those which are actually *stated.* The *audience* understands the speech or the actions of characters, but the characters themselves do not understand them. This idea of having the audience know or understand more about the situation of the characters than the characters themselves understand leads, obviously, to a number of artistic possibilities. For example, the audience knows throughout *Twelfth Night* that Viola is a girl disguised as a boy, but most of the characters in the play do not know this. The Duke earnestly pleads with Viola, whom, as his page, he calls Cesario, to help him in his wooing. The audience is constantly amused by the Duke's "knowledge gap." Viola can turn to the audience, perhaps with a wink, and say:

> I'll do my best
> To woo your lady. (*Aside*) Yet, a barful strife!
> Whoe'er I woo, myself would be his wife.
>
> (I.v.40–42)

The irony of this situation (see *mixed identity,* p. 112) is *extended.* Sometimes irony is briefer. For example, the *audience* knows that Hamlet is planning to show King Claudius' guilt by putting on a small play (the play within the play) in which events similar to those surrounding Claudius' murder of Hamlet's father occur; Claudius, however, does not suspect the plot. The difference between what the audience knows and what the king knows provides the dramatic irony. When the king asks Hamlet, "What do you call the play?" and Hamlet replies, "The Mousetrap" (III.ii.246–247), the audience, but *not* the king, realizes that Hamlet is saying that he hopes to catch the king in his trap. As the king watches the play within the play, and therein sees a murder being performed which mirrors his own murder of Hamlet's father, he rises nervously and asks to have the lights turned on. The irony is over; it has been used successfully by Shakespeare to heighten the emotional representation of Hamlet's desire for revenge (which has a definite and necessary cruelty) and Claudius' guilt.

Dramatic irony takes other forms. Sometimes a dramatist employs *ironic deeds,* that is, makes characters perform certain acts because they believe that those acts will produce certain results —when in fact the deeds produce different results. Sometimes a dramatist uses *unconscious* verbal irony, which, as we have suggested, means that a character does *not* grasp the meaning of what he is saying. When *conscious* verbal irony is being used, the character who is speaking knows the meaning of what he is saying, though he also knows that certain *other* characters do not. Hamlet, for example, is using conscious verbal irony, because *he* knows what he means when he says "mousetrap" (he knows that the audience will know what he means, but that the king will not). When Duke Orsino tells Viola that he thinks *him* prettier than most *boys,* he is using *unconscious* verbal irony; he does not know—though the audience does—the meaning of what he is saying. Sometimes a dramatist relies on various patterns of irony so *extensively* that we use the phrase *Sophoclean irony* to describe it, implying that the dramatist uses ironic deeds, and conscious and unconscious verbal irony, to the same enormous extent that Sophocles used them in his plays, particularly in *Oedipus Rex.*

Dramatic irony leads to all sorts of entertaining situations—both of a delightful nature and of a pessimistic one. When we turn to specific kinds of plays, we will see some of the ways in which irony works in comedies and in tragedies, as well as some ways in which irony tends to characterize certain comedies and tragedies, and to distinguish them from one another. Comedy, as a broad genre, ranges from the biting *satire* of plays which are heavy in irony, to the lightheartedness of plays which have only a little irony and are thus closer to comic *romance.* For now, let us simply be alert to the various forms of dramatic irony, and realize that the dramatist is exercising artistic choices when he uses any one of them. Furthermore, we should remember that verbal utterance and gesture are intimately connected in instances of conscious verbal irony. That is, when characters use conscious verbal irony, we must imagine them on stage; this is part of our understanding of dramatic art.

PATHOS. Pathos, that quality which moves the audience to pity, tenderness, or sorrow, is often generated by a helpless character or a dramatic situation in which a character is being victimized. Actually, there is a specific dramatic genre known as "pathetic tragedy" in which the hero or heroine is intentionally made overly pathetic; as the audience's feelings of pity deepen, they border on sentimental excess. Pathos is operative in most tragedies because the audience feels the tragic hero sinking deeper and deeper into some kind of psychological or physical abyss. The technique of pathos is not as easy to control as one might expect, largely because of the quantitative factor: less than that which is necessary to move the audience to feelings of pity may become static or inoperative; more than that which is needed leads to *bathos* (excessive pathos), which produces the wrong reaction in the audience (and frequently a very cynical response to the entire play—"this is just too much," etc.). The dramatist, as an artist, must therefore try to produce precisely the amount of pathos needed to secure the desired audience response.

MISTAKEN IDENTITY. Some dramatists use the device of *mistaken identity* as the mainspring of the entire plot, while others use it for passing, episodic interest and irony. When the audience knows who someone really is, but some of the characters do not, irony results. In Shakespeare's *Twelfth Night*, as we have mentioned, the girl Viola is thought to be a boy page, Cesario; her sustained double identity, or identity which is mistaken by some people in the play, produces considerable humor. The rich humor of Oliver Goldsmith's *She Stoops to Conquer* relies extensively on expert manipulation of mistaken identity. Consider what happens in this play: Marlow and Hastings are sent, by way of Tony Lumpkin's trickery, to the *residence* of Sir Richard Hardcastle believing that it is simply an *inn*. Marlow thus treats Hardcastle as the innkeeper (when in fact he is a good friend of Marlow's father who had been expecting these young guests). Hardcastle does not realize that he is being taken for an innkeeper, so he assumes that Marlow is extremely rude and uncivil. The humor of this mixed identity is deepened as Goldsmith introduces us to Hardcastle's daughter, Kate, whom Marlow of course takes to be a common bar wench. He can romance her and yet swear that he has not professed love to Kate Hardcastle (and he is not lying, because he did not realize that the girl he thought was a barmaid was really Kate). The entire play, in short, evolves from basic misunderstanding: characters do not know who the others are, and thus their behavior becomes ludicrously inappropriate.

Broad Dramatic Conventions

Drama differs in form from other kinds of literature and operates within the context of several broad conventions (that is, agreements between the dramatist and his audience). For example, the audience generally accepts almost *any* fictional device the playwright is using to advance the plot or deepen characterization. In some plays characters speak in verse. The audience knows that people in the real world do not speak in verse, but it is perfectly willing to allow the dramatist to have them do so in this play. Dryden justifies the use of verse by saying it represents real nature wrought to a higher pitch (in his *Essay of Dramatic Poesy*). The dramatist writing a verse drama does not need to worry about the audience's reaction, because both dramatist and audience accept the conventionality of dramatic speech. The characters in a Molière play, for example, those in *Le Misanthrope,* speak in poetic couplets which entertain the audience with verbal wit. The audience enjoys the rhymes (particularly, say, of Richard Wilbur's English translation of *Le Misanthrope*).

Another broad convention of drama is that a play be only a certain length—it cannot exceed an evening's entertainment. Granted, some plays are very long (*Hamlet, The Iceman Cometh*), while others are quite short (*Tom Thumb, Manfred*), but all plays have a kind of outer limit on their length because they are written to be performed in theatres before audiences who inevitably must go home. Also, because of the time limitation the dramatist can not usually spend a concentrated, in-depth amount of time on each of his characters. The audience knows this and tries to bridge to the character's depth, thereby allowing a character to acquire a complexity relatively quickly. A novelist may take several hundred pages to produce the same feeling in his reader, but he is working with different conventions.

As there are conventional limits on time, so too there is a conventional limitation of *place*. We give the dramatist freedom to suggest his location in any number of ways. As we have already mentioned, the audience allows the stage to be Rome and then Alexandria in successive scenes of *Antony and Cleopatra*. The dramatist relies on the audience's imagination to overcome the technical difficulty of having the stage represent, often with minimal change, several different places.

In addition to these few broad conventions, which govern the audience's feelings about the stage setting and the way in which characters speak, there are conventions which govern specific kinds of plays. It seems logical at this point, then, to begin our consideration of different kinds of plays, paying attention to some specific conventions and to creative ways of "breaking with" them.

What Kinds of Drama Are There?

In order to appreciate the kinds of drama which exist, it is necessary to think first of the origins of drama as we understand them. Drama evolved from certain religious ceremonies. Though there is some critical controversy at present, it is generally believed that *Greek tragedy* arose from certain Dionysian rites of life and death, while *Greek comedy* arose from certain Dionysian rites of fertility. Tragedy, then, from its beginnings, was concerned specifically with the problems of death, and comedy with the problems of fertility (and therefore with love and sex).

Before considering tragedy and comedy more specifically, let us first note what happened to drama over the ages. Greek comedy has been divided, chronologically, into three subgroups: *Old Comedy, Middle Comedy*, and *New Comedy*. Old Comedy, best illustrated by the plays of Aristophanes, included harsh political satire. New Comedy, best illustrated by the plays of Menander, generally included light humor (less biting satire), and romantic love. This new comedy of Greece was soon imitated by the writers of Roman Comedy (Plautus, Terence, *et al.*). During the Middle Ages, Rome declined as an empire and thus her influence, in the arts and otherwise, was greatly diminished. Drama became obscure, infrequent, and its evolution as an art form was arrested.

Eventually drama was given new life through the church. In the late ninth and tenth centuries there were a number of *tropes* or musical celebrations (presentations) of church services. When the priests *singing* in these tropes began to *talk* as well as to sing, a new kind of church drama evolved. Tropes became less a reflection of specific church services and more a form of dramatic entertainment; eventually, liturgical features were dropped, though religious subjects were still the most numerous. The production of these extended tropes or small plays shifted from within the church's walls to outside in the churchyard, and then to the center of the town where a larger "popular" audience applauded vigorously. This was how *medieval drama* began. The Latin of the church was exchanged for the popular vernacular, and soon there were *mystery plays* dramatizing familiar Biblical events (for example, the birth of Christ, the Crucifixion). Mystery plays led to *morality plays* in which allegorical characters were introduced in order to dramatize relationships among abstract qualities like sinfulness, conscience, redemption, virtue, and vice. Morality plays led to *interludes*, short "court entertainments" which tended to *secularize* drama. Farce was introduced. Witty dialogue came to the fore. Drama, which had begun with pagan religious rites in Greece, and then had been utilized by church liturgy, was finally becoming, by the end of the Middle Ages, an independent secular form of exciting entertainment and therefore making a claim on the artistic concerns of the people at large. The whole history of drama, then, is a distinct evolution away from religious celebration toward popular entertainment. The backgrounds of comedy and tragedy and the secularization of drama exist in and behind every play. Let us look now at the specific nature of certain basic kinds of plays, and then move further along the historical spectrum to other kinds of plays such as Elizabethan revenge tragedy and Restoration comedy.

Greek Tragedy

The dimensions and "requirements" of Greek tragedy have been clearly explained in Aristotle's famous discussion of them in his *Poetics*. *Tragedy*, according to Aristotle, is an *imitation* of *an action of high importance*. The central character, or *tragic hero*, has a particular *tragic flaw* (Aristotle's word *hamartia* is still used to discuss the flaw) which in one way or another leads to his undoing. That is, the tragic hero may make some kind of mistake through an error in judgment, or he may have some vice (*hubris*, or pride, for example) which *prevents* him from acting the *right* way. Sometimes the tragic hero falls through an understandable mishap, and sometimes through some serious flaw in his nature—he may even have a particular *virtue in excess*, and thus the virtue becomes a flaw. The tragic hero usually is led into death or despair through this important flaw or error. The hero of a Greek tragedy suffers, but usually the suffering leads to some sort of insight or wisdom, and even at the moment of his death the tragic hero seems to have an enlarged understanding of himself and his life. A flaw induces suffering, but the suffering generates wisdom. The experience of Greek tragedy is thus of a positive nature.

Aristotle also discussed the relationship between Greek tragedy and the audience. The play should have a *catharsis*, or *purgative* effect. The audience is meant to suffer *with* the tragic hero, to experience pity and fear, and thereby to be purged of those two emotions. Furthermore, by suffering with the tragic hero the audience can learn what the tragic hero learns. In order to be sure that we understand both the principles of Greek tragedy and the classical structure of tragedy, let us briefly examine *Antigone*, one of seven surviving tragedies (out of well over a hundred which were written) by Sophocles (see *Sophoclean irony*, p. 111). *Antigone* is a fairly representative Greek tragedy. The tragic hero brings death upon himself because of a tragic flaw (*hamartia*) which in this case is pride (*hubris*). The structure of the play is divided into introduction, rising action, climax, falling action, and catastrophe.

In the introduction of *Antigone* the audience is told that Creon, the new king of Thebes, has declared a law stating that the body of Polyneices may not be buried, but instead must lie in the open air and rot. Polyneices has defied the law of his banishment and is thus being severely punished, though his brother Eteocles, who has just died while trying to defend his country, has been given an honorable burial. The sister to these two brothers, the title character Antigone, wants Polyneices buried. She tries futilely to convince her sister Ismene to help her. This, then, is the opening "situation" of the play. Creon's stubborn and vain pride prevents him from allowing a decent burial for Polyneices; this, in turn, alienates Antigone, whose death will lead to deaths in Creon's own family.

In the rising action, Antigone makes a sortie out to bury the body of her brother Polyneices. At the same time, Creon makes a public announcement that the body must not be touched. This twofold rising action, then, presents the clash of interests, or conflict, which must be resolved. The climax of the play arrives when news is brought that the body of Polyneices has in fact been buried. The proud Creon almost immediately sentences Antigone to death and then accuses unjustly, of course, her sister Ismene as an accomplice in the deed. Creon's stubborn will is pitted against that of his own son, Haimon, who prophesizes that when Antigone dies, someone else will die. This prophecy is paralleled by a further prediction by Tiresias of forthcoming disaster. The last element of the falling action (the section between climax and catastrophe) is Creon's attempt to change his decree. But this attempt is futile. Creon has been too proud; suffering both for himself and for others has been generated by his mistake, or tragic flaw.

As in most Greek tragedies, catastrophe arrives in the form of death. The audience is told that Antigone has hung herself. It is conventional, in Greek tragedy for deaths to be *reported* rather than actually *depicted* on stage; the reporting is made by a *nuntius* (Latin for messenger), who arrives and announces the event. Then the audience is *told* that Creon's son Haimon, who had challenged his father and predicted death, thrust at his father with a sword and, missing him, turned it on himself. Creon returns to Thebes carrying the dead body of his son, only to find that even more unhappiness awaits him. Soon he (and of course the audience) *hears* that his wife, Eurydice, has stabbed herself and cursed Creon as she died. Thus three deaths have been *reported* (Antigone's, Haimon's, and Eurydice's). This triple death constitutes the catastrophe of the play and the ironic reward (see *reversal*, p. 91) for a proud man who had stubbornly forbidden the burial of Polyneices. The play is heavy with Sophoclean irony; events not only lead to unexpected results, but they do so with a kind of vicious poetic justice. The play began, after all, with a refusal to have someone buried, that is, with a conflict over death. This conflict led to further death in the end; the question of burial becomes quite small beside the question of living.

As is customary in Greek tragedy, the chorus delivers the final word. When Creon enters his house at the end of the play the chorus explains that in order to secure happiness one must have wisdom, but sometimes wisdom arrives too late, or only *after* suffering. Creon is "educated" by his experience, and his wisdom at the end is entirely valid. But his earlier ignorance, which took the form of pride, led to great unhappiness. Early in the play Creon defied the gods, and in the end he was punished by them. The events of the play are worked out within the conventional structure of introduction, rising action, climax, falling action, and catastrophe. (Students might try to remember the structure of Sophocles' *Antigone*, its characters, conflict, tragic hero, etc., in order to have a quick basis for comparing other tragedies and a *representative Greek tragedy*.)

Greek Comedy

Greek comedy developed, as we have noted, from early pagan fertility rites. The *earliest* Greek comedies also were concerned with phallic rites, and comedy since then has generally contained a sexual element (though never becoming blatantly oversexual in its focus). We have also noted the conventional division of Greek comedy into three categories: *Old Comedy, Middle Comedy,* and *New Comedy.* Old Comedy, which is best represented by Aristophanes' three plays, *The Frogs, The Clouds,* and *The Birds,* usually concerns itself with matters of state and therefore contains a generous amount of political satire. Middle Comedy, unfortunately, has no *surviving* plays. It is a form of drama we know about, but not firsthand. New Comedy, probably best represented by the humorous plays of Menander (born around 342 B.C., or about forty years after Aristophanes died), focused on what has become a convention of comedy as we think of it today, namely, the "happy ending." New Comedy usually told a story about romantic love (expressing indirectly the history of early comedy and its associations with fertility and sexuality). Usually in these comedies we find a certain problem, generally one which entangles the lives of would-be young lovers. In the course of the play the problem is solved, and a happy ending results.

If all of this sounds terribly pleasant, it is. Comedy, in general, is exciting, entertaining, and happy. Comedy has light subject matter, a hero who is usually victorious, and a mood which is airy and optimistic (in contrast to tragedy, where the subject matter is heavy, the hero usually unsuccessful, and a mood which is somber and dark). Unfortunately Aristotle's detailed theories on the nature of comedy are lost to us. What comments we do have are few and brief. He notes in the *Poetics* that comedy is an *imitation* of characters of a *lower* class, not so much villainous as *ludicrous* figures, whom Aristotle considered a subdivision of people who are ugly or base. Ludicrous characters were those whose baseness and ugliness were not particularly painful or destructive. They were generally either buffoons, ironical, or simply imposters. The language of comedy was "low," and the diction generally popular.

Aristotle talked more about tragedy, as we have seen, than about comedy, because he felt that comedy was not, at least at first, treated seriously as art. Comedy was late in being granted a regular chorus by the Archon, and for some time those who played parts in comedies did so strictly on a voluntary basis.

From such other ancient documents as we have, which manifest a familiarity with Aristotle's further thoughts about comedy, we generally are inclined to think that comedy—in addition to being an imitation of a ludicrous action and in addition to leading to *derisive* laughter (the audience is made to feel superior to the characters)—was supposed to *purge* the audience of *pleasure* and *laughter;* laughter, it is said, was the *mother of comedy.* Old Comedy was thought to be very funny, New Comedy a little less so, and Middle Comedy a kind of combination of both.

Old Comedy and New Comedy were somewhat less stereotyped than Greek tragedy. With the intention of producing laughter rather than the more serious emotions of pity and fear, comedy tended to follow structural patterns up to a point—and then launch into a kind of final, antiorganizational section. Students today are inclined to be assigned Old Comedies, partially because there are better surviving texts, but also because it is perhaps easier to see them as the greater sources of much modern comedy. Greek New Comedy can best be understood by examining some of the later Roman imitators—and particularly the plays of Plautus and Terence. To understand Old Comedy, we may take a brief look at Aristophanes' *The Clouds.*

As with Greek tragedy, Greek Old Comedy has a definite structural pattern: *prologos, parados, agon, parabasis,* and a final less organized section, generally a farcical sort of conclusion.

In *The Clouds,* the *prologos,* or formal opening of the play, is taken up with presenting the audience with the main problem, how the father-figure, Strepsiades, can learn the way to evade his creditors and avoid paying his old debts. Next comes the *parados* (parade) at which point the chorus marches in, usually with all of the members dressed as animals in wild, exciting costumes. In *The Clouds* the parade is a chorus of *clouds* dressed in dew and varying in hue and shape. They are addressed as goddesses by Socrates, the Greek philosopher being satirized in the play (because of the basic rivalry between philosophers and poets to be the teachers of their society). Strepsiades is impressed by the chorus of clouds and, with Socrates' encouragement, sees in it a potential form of forthcoming aid in solving his problem of debt evasion. Next comes the *agon,* or debate between some forces over the problem or over a related problem that we have been informed about in the *prologos*. Usually this *agon* precedes the *parabasis* (coming-forward), in which the dramatist comes forth, through his chorus, and directly addresses the audience for the first time. In *The Clouds*, however, Aristophanes reversed this order: the *parabasis* precedes the *agon*. In the *parabasis* the chorus speaks for the poet. It begins, "O Spectators," and uses such phrases as "I the poet." The poet tells the audience how he labors to please them and expresses his hope that they will applaud this play as they have recently applauded its predecessor. He claims that he always has fresh ideas and novel jests in his plays, and then satirically calls on the gods to lend strength to his choral song, noting (conventionally) that poets have not been treated as well as they should be. The chorus' speech is brought to an end as Socrates enters, complaining of the stupidity of his new pupil, Strepsiades, who, of course, is trying to learn how to avoid paying his debts.

Shortly, the *agon* or debate arrives, in this case a humorous, satirical debate between Right Logic and Wrong Logic; before this debate begins, however, there is a good bit of humorous stage discussion of Strepsiades' problem. Strepsiades suggests, for example, that he could perhaps conjure the moon into coming down, and then lock it in a box. If the moon were thus trapped, there could be no passing of the days, and thus no interest could accrue on his unpaid debts. This humor is quite typical of "Aristophanic wit" and lies at the center, really, of what is actually funny about Old Comedy. The chorus counsels Strepsiades to send his son to do the learning, since he, Strepsiades, is such a poor pupil! Pheidippides, Strepsiades' son, thinks his father is going crazy, especially because he has faith in a lunatic like the mad-brained Socrates (the object of Aristophanes' satire), and wonders, for example, whether he should indict his father for lunacy or simply tell the undertakers about his symptoms. The *agon* ensues, bringing to an end the formal parts of the play. As Right and Wrong Logic exit, Socrates enters from the school where he has been teaching Strepsiades' son, and Strepsiades comes to inquire how his son is doing, only to be told by Socrates that he can make a sophist out of him yet. The play proceeds to deal with the original problem. In the end, Strepsiades' efforts come to naught and his son has learned to prove by logic that it is right to beat a father and a mother. The chorus tells Strepsiades it serves him right to have turned to wicked practices (consulting with a philosopher), and that he had been a mad fool to have cast away his gods for Socrates. The audience is laughing, because the silly Strepsiades has been led to a silly undoing. Comic justice prevails and foolish people are, in the end, ridiculed.

It is not hard to see the basic differences between comedy and tragedy as they existed in their earliest Greek forms in plays like *The Clouds* and *Antigone*. The characters of the one are low, of the other high; the diction and language are slangy and entirely popular in comedy; in tragedy the language is usually lofty and rhetorical; the conclusion of a comedy is funny and provokes final laughter; the conclusion of tragedy is sad and provokes final pity and fear; in comedy, ludicrous characters are led, in their ignorance, to ludicrous ends, whereas in tragedy serious characters are led, often through the tragic hero's ignorance, or "tragic flaw," to serious ends.

At the same time it should be noted that there are also qualities and characteristics which comedies and tragedies share or have in common. Both depend on plot. Both deal with relationships between man and society. Tragic heroes usually strive to achieve things beyond the reach of ordinary men, and in their "overreaching" are usually led to disaster or death. The leading characters in comedy are usually foolish and ludicrous, like Strepsiades or like the title character of Molière's *Le Misanthrope*. But in both, the protagonists are suffering in their own particular ways and are trying to overcome some kind of problem. Thus both comedies and tragedies have a broad structural organization of moving from problem to solution.

We have seen in Old Comedy that there is much harsh satire; in *The Clouds* we discover a biting attack on Socrates in particular and philosophers in general. The play deliberately appeals to logic, for science seems hopelessly inadequate for man's basic, everyday needs. Aristophanes quite seriously believed that man, as he experiences this world, should have more fruitful, human activity. He should avoid the endless pseudoscientific rigamorole of the philosophers. *The Clouds* was performed in 423 B.C., and contemporaries recognized and accepted as wicked satire the play's biting portrait of Socrates. Roughly a generation later, in 399 B.C., Socrates was denied freedom of speech, because his society had come to believe that he really *was* the foolish character of the play. The point is that Old Comedy, with its expressly political satire and attacks, has an inherent seriousness and a capacity for propaganda that can result in lasting damage (that is, the undeserved death of Socrates).

In contrast to the fantastic elements (chorus of clouds, a utopia of birds, etc.) and the harsh satire of Old Comedy, in New Comedy we discover playful romantic love and humorous romantic entanglements (recall that in between Old Comedy and New Comedy there was Middle Comedy, but that no surviving examples have been found). New Comedy was experimented with by Menander (343?–291? B.C.), and then used later as the basis for Roman Comedy, that is, for the New Comedies written by the Roman playwrights Plautus (254?–184 B.C.) and Terence (190?–159? B.C.). Both of these playwrights were to have a large influence on the development of English drama. As an example of New Comedy we can examine briefly Plautus' *Menechmi*, or *The Menechmus Twins*. This play served as the source and model for Shakespeare's *The Comedy of Errors*, and certainly Shakespeare's title may stand as an apt summary of the essential nature of New Comedy (and, later, of much *romantic comedy*).*

In Plautus' play there are twin brothers, both with the name Menechmus, the first a citizen of Epidamnum and the second a traveler from Syracuse. This latter brother arrives in Epidamnum and is, of course, mistaken for his twin brother. The second

* An English translation of Plautus' Latin play was printed in 1595, and our first recorded mention of Shakespeare's play appeared at Christmas time in 1594 in the notebooks of some law students. Thus it is not absolutely clear whether Shakespeare had read the translation or not, though some phrases suggest that he had. It is also entirely possible that the translator (a "W.W." not yet further identified) read Shakespeare's play first! Shakespeare most likely studied Latin at school and may very well have read *Menechmi* in the original or later versions.

Menechmus has a slave, Messenio, who becomes confused with the parasite, Peniculus. The main joke arrives when the mistress of Epidamnum, Erotium, gives a gold chain to his twin brother accidentally. When Epidamnum asks her for it, she gets very angry and says she has already given it to him! Unable to understand why his wife is behaving in such a strange way, Epidamnum goes to ask advice from his friends. There are other humorous episodes, all revolving around the *mistaken identity* (see p. 112). Every time the brother, who is the traveler, meets someone, he is taken for his brother (for whom he is searching, this being the reason he came to this town in the first place). Finally, as one might expect, the Menechmus twins meet and recognize each other. Both are delighted—as is the audience—and the brother from Syracuse asks his new-found brother to come back to Syracuse for a visit. Menechmus of Epidamnum consents and all ends happily. The play is filled with good jokes, all connecting to the central misunderstanding which wives, masters, physicians, and others share. The problem of the play is easily resolved by having the twin brothers meet. There is a great deal of laughter and broad humor throughout the play and a generally light playfulness.

Shakespeare made some modifications on Plautus' play, but the main outline is still the same. One interesting change which Shakespeare wrought was to have each of the twin brothers have a slave who was *also* a twin to the other's slave, thus complicating matters even further. Thus the law students who mentioned the Shakespearean production in 1594 called it *The Night of Errors*. Shakespeare's play, written early in his career, is not one of his best. The diction is frequently weak, the wit excessive, and the gimmicks occasionally tiring. Nevertheless, as farce, as the epitome of ludicrous human activity and cause for laughter, it comes very close to being the perfect example of what comedy was designed to be, festive and mirthful.

Nicholas Udall, the early sixteenth-century dramatist, wrote a comedy entitled *Ralph Roister Doister* which, as its title might suggest, was quite definitely a ludicrous farce. Udall certainly had Plautus and Terence in mind when he wrote his "Prologue" to the play, two stanzas of which follow:

For mirth prolongeth life, and causeth health;
  Mirth recreates our spirits, and voideth pensiveness;
Mirth increaseth amity, not hindering our wealth;
  Mirth is to be used both of more and less,
  Being mixed with virtue in decent comeliness—
As we trust no good nature can gainsay the same:
Which mirth we intend to use, avoiding all blame.

The wise poets long time heretofore
  Under merry comedies secrets did declare,
Whereine was contained very virtuous lore,
  With mysteries and forewarnings very rare.
  Such to write neither Plautus nor Terence did spare,
Which among the learned at this day bears the bell:
These with such other therein did excell.

One of the most fascinating aspects of drama is its constant change. Granted, Greek tragedy was identifiable as such (and we will look, shortly, at other kinds of tragedies which it spawned). And our examination of a Greek Old Comedy and a Roman New Comedy shows the entirely plastic nature of comedy and indeed "the comic." For if the goal is to make people laugh, there is simply no limit to the dramatist's attempts to show the foolish, the ludicrous, and the laughable. One of the best comments on the lack of codified "rules" for comedy is that well-known and sometimes anthologized discussion of comedy presented in Ben Jonson's 1599 comedy, *Every Man Out of His Humour;* a portion of that discussion follows:

MITIS. You have seen his play, Cordatus? Pray you, how is't?
CORDATUS. Faith, sir, I must refrain to judge. Only this I can say of it: 'tis strange, and of a particular kind by itself, somewhat like Vetus Comoedia; work that hath bounteously pleased me, how it will answer the general expectation I know not.
MITIS. Does he observe all the laws of comedy in it?
CORDATUS. What laws mean you?
MITIS. Why, the equal division of it into acts, and scenes, according to the Terentian manner; his true number of actors; the furnishing of the scene with Grex, of chorus; and that

the whole argument fall within compass of a day's business.

CORDATUS. O no, these are too nice observations.

MITIS. They are such as must be received, by your favour, or it cannot be authentic.

CORDATUS. Troth, I can discern no such necessity.

MITIS. No?

CORDATUS. No, I assure you, signior. If those laws you speak of had been delivered us, ab initio, and in their present virtue and perfection, there had been some reason of obeying their powers. But 'tis extant that that which we call Comoedia was at first nothing but a simple and continued song, sung by one only person, till Susario invented a second; after him, Epicharmus a third; Phormus and Chionides devised to have four actors, with a prologue and chorus; to which Cratinus, long after, added a fifth and sixth; Eupolis, more; Aristophanes, more than they; every man, in the dignity of his spirit and judgment, supplied something. And though that in him this kind of poem appeared absolute and fully perfected, yet how is the face of it changed since, in Menander, Philemon, Cecilius, Plautus, and the rest; who have utterly excluded the chorus, altered the property of the persons, their names and natures, and augmented it with all liberty, according to the elegancy and disposition of those times wherein they wrote. I see not, then, but we should enjoy the same license, or free power, to illustrate and heighten our invention as they did; and not be tied to these strict and regular forms, which the niceness of a few—who are nothing but form—would thrust upon us.

This discussion, from Jonson's Induction (formal introduction), emphasizes not only that different comedians have changed the nature of comedy—that Plautus, say, had traveled some distance since comedy was simply the song of a single person—but also that past changes prepare us for future ones. To be a vital form, comedy must keep undergoing modifications. The same holds true for tragedy. Because drama is written to be performed, it needs to be very *immediate*. Drama changes in society and thus in the audience. In 1968, for example, when the demand for *audience participation* in the play mushroomed, a number of plays, like *Dionysus in 69*, had as their goal the integration of their audience, and one play, *Paradise Now*, induced members of the audience (including an important drama critic) to throw off their clothes as a dramatic gesture of participation in Paradise. Changes in society have, in the past, led to some very interesting kinds of tragedies and comedies. As we turn to look at some of them now, we should try to remember that comedy is not all funny and that tragedy is not all sad. Some comedies have a seriousness about them, particularly perhaps those comedies which have the protagonist punished by his society because of his difference or defect—Jonson's Volpone, Molière's Alceste, etc. And many tragedies have "comic relief," events which are essentially funny and thus serve to interrupt or mitigate the tension being generated by the more serious dimension of the play. Both comedy and tragedy, in other words, borrow from each other to a certain extent, and this will be seen as we look at further kinds of plays.

Senecan and Elizabethan Tragedy

When we think of *Elizabethan tragedy* we are, really, thinking of several kinds of plays, all of which developed with considerable genius during Elizabeth's reign. Early Elizabethan tragedy was modeled on the Latin tragedies of Seneca (4 B.C.?–A.D. 65) which were frequently read in the schools and which gained in popularity during the years 1559–1581 (most critics feel that before 1580 there was no real interest in tragedy in England).

Senecan tragedy had certain distinguishing characteristics which are important to bear in mind: modeled primarily on the Greek tragedies of Euripides, they had a five-act division, made use of a chorus and certain stock characters (ghost, female confidante, cruel tyrant, etc.), presented most of the action through narrative reports (recall our mention of the messenger, or *nuntius*), centered on "sensational" themes of bloody murder and destructive cruelty (often using the motive of *revenge* as the "exciting action"), made use of a bombastic, highly rhetorical style filled with hyperbole, and, finally, used numerous soliloquies.

As might be expected, these various characteristics added up to something more than the tragedies of Euripides. Senecan tragedy can be thought of as an enormous modification and embellishment of Greek tragedy, with the main change being in the direction of an action and an idiom of sensationalism. Seneca's nine tragedies were translated and acted with some frequency among boys' schools, though the English plays modeled on Seneca's were, undoubtedly, of greater popular interest.

The first English tragedy of this period was Sackville and Norton's *Gorbuduc.** Both writers used blank verse, for the first time in English drama, and followed Seneca's example in having the speeches of the chorus separate the acts. This play was followed by other Senecan imitations like *Jocasta* (acted 1566) and *The Misfortunes of Arthur* (1588). Other early Senecan tragedies were written by a small literary group, headed by the Countess of Pembroke, sister of the poet Sir Philip Sidney, and her followers (all of whom were imitating the French Senecan plays of Robert Garnier). These early Senecan plays did not have an enormous influence, at least not compared with the later ones which led directly to what most people think of as Elizabethan tragedy. It was Thomas Kyd (1588–1594) and, shortly later, Christopher Marlowe (1564–1593), who advanced tragedy as a genre with exciting dimensions. Most famous and most influential in the development of later Senecan (Elizabethan) tragedy was Kyd's *The Spanish Tragedy.*

This play opens with the ghost of Andrea talking with Revenge (personified). This induction does not establish precisely how Andrea was killed; in the first act, however, we learn that he was killed (slaughtered, really) by Balthazar, the son of the Viceroy of Portugal. Andrea left behind him his lady-love Bel-imperia, and his good friend Horatio. The latter begins a romance with Bel-imperia—who is also loved by the jealous Balthazar. Balthazar arranges to have Bel-imperia's servant, Pedringano, slaughter and hang Horatio. This leads to great grief for Horatio's father, Hieronimo, the Marshall of Spain, and Horatio's mother, Isabella. Hieronimo is anxious for revenge. The murder of Horatio thus takes place soon after Balthazar and his friend Lorenzo had spied

* The first three acts are generally thought of as written by Thomas Norton and the last two acts by Thomas Sackville. Both men were members of Parliament, and the play was presented before Queen Elizabeth in 1562.

on Horatio and Bel-imperia professing love in the garden. Pedringano is hung for the murder of Horatio, because Lorenzo does not keep his promise to secure his release. Eventually, in Act IV (there are four acts, which was typical of Seneca's tragedies), Hieronimo induces everyone to participate in a play and enlists the aid of Bel-imperia. The play within the play is a "Spanish tragedy" and the actors portraying the characters within it to be killed are themselves actually killed: Bel-imperia stabs Prince Balthazar in the middle of the play, Hieronimo kills the Duke of Castille and his son. Other murders are, of course, in the background: Horatio had been murdered; Bel-imperia dies, and Hieronimo kills himself. The play becomes a massive depiction of slayings, suicides, and hangings. Revenge provides the impetus for spectacle. Conspiracies, underhanded murders, and general enmity abound.

Many of the Senecan devices had been firmly established by the time Kyd wrote this play, and thus we find him using the play within the play, the dumb show, garden scenes, the chorus, the ghost, the bloody murders, and general spectacle. However, as numerous critics have noted, Kyd made certain innovations which have had a lasting effect on tragedy: he abandoned the general reliance on a story from classical mythology or ancient Britain and instead used a modern story set in Spain; he made his plot more elaborate and added multiple subplots; he focused on the psychological *disorders* of characters, thus moving away from *roles* toward *individuals;* he invented a great amount of "stage business," or the general hustle-and-bustle activity designed to increase the audience's feeling of active involvement in a distinctive, identifiable world. He also relied heavily on dramatic soliloquy to aid in characterization (see *soliloquy,* p. 99), and thus went well beyond the rather sparse soliloquies to be found in Senecan drama. Indeed, it has been argued with considerable force that the basic popularity of Kyd's play was due not to the sensational and exciting subject matter but to the eloquence of Hieronimo's brooding, high-pitched soliloquies lamenting his son's death and planning for his revenge.

Kyd's broadening of basic Senecan drama led to the tragedies of Marlowe and then to those of Shakespeare. Generally, this later tragedy was considered *romantic tragedy*, having wider scope or larger subject matter than either Senecan or Greek tragedy, and also possessing a greater concern for psychological development of character (the Elizabethan audiences were particularly fascinated with personality disorders). Romantic tragedy, which was really perfected by Shakespeare, also had a looser structure and a greater inclusion of both the comic and the horrible. Senecan tragedy, in other words, led to a broader kind of tragedy than the original classical tragedy epitomized by *Oedipus Rex* and *Antigone*.

There also developed a particular kind of tragedy known as the *chronicle play*, a kind of drama which drew its subject matter from various chronicles of English history (see *chronicle play*, p. 135), and a kind of tragedy known as *bourgeois* or *domestic*. This was tragedy based on the drama of ordinary life and was first given form in *Arden of Feversham* (1592), a tragedy which dramatized the actual murder of a town's leading citizen. Let us turn now to a closer consideration of bourgeois or domestic tragedy.

Domestic Tragedy

For the most part, tragedies produced between the time of the Greek tragedians and the middle of the sixteenth century dealt with heroes of high station in society. This, of course, was one of Aristotle's requirements for tragedy, implicit in his principle that the hero of a tragedy must fall, through some flaw (*hamartia*), from a *high degree*. There are numerous medieval references to this idea—many in Chaucer's poetry, for example—and it was not until the English Renaissance that a few dramatists began to write a new kind of tragedy, having as its hero an *ordinary* man (that is, *not* from a high station), and thus called *bourgeois* or *domestic* tragedy. The idea of the middle-class hero is used well in Thomas Heywood's *A Woman Killed with Kindness* (1607). This play was extremely popular with the bourgeois of Heywood's day and has also been well received on the modern stage.

As Heywood's play has, since its appearance, been considered "representative of domestic tragedy," it is worth taking note of what happens. There are two plots, a main plot and a subplot (something we will see frequently as we survey kinds of plays). Let us focus on the main plot. Master John Frankford has married Anne and is very happy with her. When he is required to be away on business, however, he arranges to have his trusted friend, Master Wendoll, look after Anne. Wendoll soon declares his love for Anne and she is unable to resist his charming manner. A servant—one of those "poor household spies" Ben Jonson asks his beloved Celia to hide from in Volpone's well-known song—Nicholas, sees the infidelity develop and alerts his master, Frankford. Together they make a plan to capture Anne in her sin; they make a duplicate set of keys to the house, pretend to be leaving overnight, and then sneak back inside (having left their horses quiet at a distance). Frankford discovers Anne and Wendoll in bed in each other's arms. He accuses her of sin, even before their two children (an element of *pathos*), and decides to kill her with kindness: he simply decides to make her live in his manor, with servants, but never visit or communicate with him. Before long, everyone gathers around the dying Anne. Psychologically unable to live with herself, she has stopped eating and thus is dying. Frankford pardons her on her deathbed, but the playwright suggests that if Frankford had severely punished Anne, she would have lived; instead, his kindness has killed her.

As is readily apparent, no tragic hero falls from high degree. Instead, Heywood has chosen to present the gloomy consequences of familiar marital infidelity. In a subplot we discover the loss of honor (Susan's chastity) prevented by a man's honor (Sir Francis' refusal to accept Susan as payment of a debt), and the entire play is concerned with the many varieties of problems of marital and extramarital love and sex. A wave of emotions is released. The audience feels pity and horror. Anne's death is gruesome.

Some critics feel that this kind of domestic tragedy has as much "tragic" about it as ancient Greek tragedy; other critics do not, and the debate is far from over. Domestic tragedy, in any case, has thrived. In the eighteenth century there were numerous domestic tragedies, particularly the well-known play, *Jane Shore* (1714), by Nicholas Rowe. Rowe's strong moral questioning and his focusing on the pity of the life of a mistress led to his being named England's poet laureate the following year.* Rowe's domestic tragedies were termed "sentimental," or excessive in pathos, but nevertheless they proved that middle-class people could certainly be subjects for dramatic tragedy. In more recent times, we have a good example of domestic tragedy in Arthur Miller's *Death of a Salesman.* The tragic hero of the title, Willy Loman, has certainly not fallen from high degree. Willy Loman is almost the perfect example of a middle-class tragic hero, though many others could be named, particularly, say, in the plays of Ibsen, Shaw, and O'Neill.

Heroic Drama and Heroic Tragedy

While bourgeois or domestic tragedy relies on a middle-class hero and a middle-class world, *heroic tragedy* goes to the other extreme and deals with lofty people in a lofty world. Heroic tragedy is a subdivision of the larger genre of *heroic drama,* in which the hero does not necessarily die, but is nevertheless a head of state or lofty character involved in serious, enormous passions and conflict. In heroic drama, and therefore in heroic tragedy, the characters are intentionally made "larger-than-life." They speak in lofty language about the important events of their lofty lives. The dramatic principle is that things which happen to ordinary people which seem dramatic are even *more* dramatic when they happen to "larger-than-life" characters.

While bourgeois tragedy grew up during the Renaissance, heroic tragedy was specifically the child of the Restoration (the period of 1660–1700, beginning with the "restoration" of Stuart leadership in England when Charles II came to the throne). The theaters of London had been officially closed from the autumn of 1642 until after the restoration of Charles. During this period the Puritan forces had brought inertia to the English

* Rowe was the first editor of Shakespeare after the Folios.

theater, and popular taste for roguish entertainment had consequently subsided (though during the official closing time of the theaters the lower classes nevertheless delighted in various acrobatic acts, mummings, drolls, etc.). Thus, after 1660 the theater was not the same. (And certainly it had been shattered in a quantitative sense, going from a half-dozen London playhouses at the beginning of the century to only two following the Restoration.) In the summer of 1660 the new king gave his friends, Sir William Davenant and Thomas Killigrew, a virtual monopoly in establishing actors' companies and performing plays. One group, headed by Davenant, acted after 1671 in a new theater in Dorset Garden; the other, headed by Killigrew, became known as the King's players and from 1674 on performed plays in the Theatre Royal. What did this mean? Well, obviously with the king running things behind the scenes, the theater was an entertainment primarily for the upper-class members of the court; courtiers, not businessmen, were organizing things, and the broad merchant class was excluded. Instead of evolving a popular drama for the burgeoning middle class, they evolved a drama dealing with upper-class figures. The two kinds of entertainment which became popular were *operas* and so-called heroic plays which contained considerable moral debate, introspection, debates over various competing abstract virtues and qualities, and, most specifically and frequently, debates over the value of *love* versus the value of *honor*.

The heroic play, coming out of an identifiably upper-class climate, and managed by courtiers, is, then, an example of a genre coming to life through *cultural* as well as *artistic* change. John Dryden was the master of the heroic play, and also wrote commentary about this new genre with which he and others were experimenting.* Dryden thought that "an heroic play ought to be an imitation, in little, of an heroic poem; and, consequently, that Love and Valour ought to be the subject of it."

Heroic tragedy (heroic drama with a hero who dies) is not as distinctive as the broader genre in which it participates. The

* In his well-known essay, *Of Heroic Plays*, attached as a preface to the text of his heroic play, *The Conquest of Granada* (1672), Dryden explains, qualifies, and defends the genre.

archetypal example of heroic *drama* is Dryden's *The Indian Queen* (which he wrote under collaboration with his brother-in-law). In brief, the play proceeds as follows: the general of the Inca's forces, Montezuma, wants to marry the Inca's daughter, Orazia, as his reward for conquering the Mexicans. However, because Montezuma is not of royal blood himself, he is considered ineligible for such a marriage. In the end of the play it turns out that Montezuma is in fact the son of the true Queen of Mexico, and thus is eligible to marry Orazia. In the course of the play there is considerable discussion of honor (Montezuma even changes sides and fights for the Mexicans). The other characters, from the young idealist, Acacis, to the villain-general, Traxalla, become familiar *types* in later heroic plays. In general, a heroic tragedy will have a military leader as its hero, an emperor on a foreign land, an incredibly virtuous heroine, and a nasty villain. The aspect of the play which becomes convention is the nature of the hero himself; consider, for example, Dryden's description of the hero in one of his later plays, *The Conquest of Granada:*

> Vast is his courage, boundless is his mind,
> Rough as a storm, and humorous as wind:
> Honor's the only idol of his eyes;
> The charms of beauty like a pest he flies;
> And, rais'd by valor from a birth unknown,
> Acknowledges no pow'r above his own.

This speech is characteristic of the *excesses* of heroic drama. Heroes speak of themselves—and are described by other characters—in enormous, boasting, pompous terms. Certainly we are at the other extreme from heroes like Heywood's Master Frankford and Miller's Willy Loman. In his later tragedies, Dryden continued to use the elevated hero, full-blown rhetoric, and exotic setting.

A good example of genre interaction (cross-fertilization) can be seen in Dryden's "heroic" version—*All for Love*—of Shakespeare's tragedy, *Antony and Cleopatra.* Here the heroic drama, in setting before its audience characters who are larger than life, cannot easily become fully "tragic," because of a basic inability to exhibit *human* qualities as *suffering* characters. The lack of human interest which is frequently criticized in Dryden's heroic tragedies is justified. Nevertheless, *All for Love*, like Dryden's other Shakespearean adaptation, *Troilus and Cressida*, contains some very fine language (particularly blank verse) and illustrates well the neoclassical ideal of the three *unities* (unity of place—one setting, unity of action, and unity of time—taking place within a twenty-four-hour span).

There were numerous other playwrights producing heroic tragedies and we can mention Lee, Otway, Southerne (and, perhaps, the lesser figures, Banks and Crowne); most of them were more or less blending Elizabethan tragedy with heroic drama, under the continental influence of the tragic dramatists Corneille and Racine (Corneille's plays did not adhere as strictly to the "rules" of tragedy as Racine's did). These tragedies, following Dryden's example, focused on the passions and states of mind of lofty personages, emphasized highly rhetorical accounts of feelings, and diminished external action.

Gradually, the genre of heroic tragedy moved away from extreme heroics toward a more sentimental pathos. The playwright Thomas Otway (1652–1685) began to treat his heroic characters more in the light of human beings than demi-gods, and the characters began to speak a more natural, or ordinary, language. In the successes of Otway, Lee, and Southerne, English tragedy moved away from the bombast of heroic tragedy and toward a more sincere interest in basic human nature.

The Chronicle Play

Christopher Marlowe, the Elizabethan dramatist who had the second greatest influence on the course of English drama, wrote his mighty *Tamburlaine* (Part I) in about 1587. This play had as its subject the career of the historical personage Timur. The play was extremely successful and was given popular performance by the Admiral's company of actors, whose "star" was the famous Edward Alleyn (many critics feel that Alleyn's greatness and individuality as an actor led Marlowe to write other "one-man plays" like *Doctor Faustus* and *The Jew of Malta*). Marlowe's Tamburlaine, the royal conqueror riding triumphantly through Persepolis, excited the Elizabethan audience and led to a renewed interest in historical chronicles. Thus a number of other dramatists tried to write *chronicle plays,* producing such works as *The Troublesome Reign of King John of England* (1591) in two parts. Chronicle plays also led to an interest in *bourgeois tragedy* (see p. 130), a genre best illustrated perhaps by the 1592 play *Arden of Feversham,* which took as its subject an actual murder related in Holinshed's *Chronicle* (1577).

One result of the new interest in both chronicle plays and bourgeois tragedy was the creation of an uncertainty as to *what* tragedy ought to be. Marlowe's plays tended to emphasize characterization (and usually of the main character at the expense of the others) and dramatic action, without a particular concern for the formal nature of tragedy. Marlowe's language was also extremely exciting. He used blank verse in new and dramatic ways and made particularly good use of geographical names in iambic lines, such as the often quoted line, "And ride in triumph through Persepolis" (*I Tamburlaine,* 754). Furthermore, Marlowe introduced a certain kind of new human argument into his plays. He tended to nullify a number of absolutes by pointing out, for example, that it is very *hard* for a king to know what to do in certain situations; that, in fact, it is very hard to be a king at all; that it is not absolutely clear whether Faustus was doing a terrible thing or a very human and understandable thing when he sold his soul to the devil; and that, above all, it is *man's struggle,* not his goals, which makes him exciting. This sort of thinking tended to make tragedy more *romantic,* which, as we have noted, is the term one can best apply to the tragedies of Shakespeare. Indeed, Shakespeare's own development more or less reflects his shifting away from chronicle plays (he molded the earlier two parts of the history of King John into one play, for example), to a series of different experiments, until by the end of Elizabeth's reign he was through writing history plays (excepting *King Henry VIII*). Shakespeare's early tragedies, the four written before 1603, were mostly Senecan (see *Senecan and Elizabethan drama,* p. 127), and only later did his tragedy acquire full romantic breadth in the three great plays, *Othello, Lear,* and *Macbeth.*

The chronicle play was often combined with comedy or tragedy, and certainly we are all familiar with the comedy in Shakespeare's Falstaff plays (*Henry IV* [Part I], *Henry IV* [Part II], and *Henry V*). We can also cite the blending of tragedy and history in *Richard III.* In other words, the chronicle play, which did not attract a particularly large number of dramatists, was merged into other kinds of drama with considerable influence and thus may be thought of as a catalyst to the genius of greater plays written by Marlowe and Shakespeare.

Pastoral Drama

A student interested in learning about pastoral drama should begin by reading the comments on *pastoral poetry* in the first section of this book. Pastoral drama made use of various conventions of pastoral poetry, borrowing, specifically, a pastoral landscape, rich bucolic descriptions, and at least some characters from the pastoral world. Pastoral drama developed in Italy in the sixteenth century and led to English experiments in the genre by George Peele, Samuel Daniel, John Fletcher, Ben Jonson, and others. It also led to the inclusion of pastoral elements in some of Shakespeare's romantic comedies.

Peele's early pastoral play *The Arraignment of Paris* (1584) is very typical: Paris, a handsome *shepherd,* is in love with Oenone in a *vale on Mt. Ida* (a conventional pastoral setting). Three beautiful women—Pallas, Juno (wife and sister of Jove), and Venus—come upon Paris and Oenone who are singing and *playing on a pipe* (recall the use of this pastoral convention in the best pastoral elegy in English, Milton's "Lycidas"). A large golden ball is discovered with an inscription indicating that it should be given to the fairest. As Juno, Pallas, and Venus all think themselves the fairest, they agree to have Paris be the judge. Paris chooses Venus (the goddess of love). Shortly, Mercury comes and announces that Paris has been summoned to Jove (as Jove's jealous wife Juno, who lost the contest, has requested this). In Jove's court Paris is "arraigned" or charged with having been unfair. When he explains what has happened, it is agreed that he had not acted differently than any other mortal might have acted. The gods decide to allow Diana to settle the matter. She takes the oaths of Juno, Pallas, and Venus to abide by her decision—which is, it turns out, to give the golden ball to Queen Elizabeth (thereby directly, and some think too blatantly, flattering Queen Elizabeth). The play ends happily as all accept this final decision. Peele's play contains songs, verse experiments, loose structure (which also characterized the chronicle plays), but above all, a general pastoral awareness. The chief character is a shepherd, the story fanciful and pleasant rather than philosophically profound, and the overall atmosphere is light. This lightness and the use of pastoral setting can be seen as operating with maximum effectiveness in Shakespeare's *As You Like It* (see the following discussion of *romantic comedy*).

Romantic Comedy

Romantic comedy almost always has *love* as its main subject. Furthermore, there is generally a good deal of action taking place outdoors (in forests, gardens, vales, pastoral settings). There is also a very beautiful heroine, sometimes disguised for most of the play as a man, who is pursued with considerable confusion or difficulty by several suitors. Romantic comedies, which were first fully developed on the early Elizabethan stage by Robert Greene, Thomas Dekker, Shakespeare, and others, generally exhibit a debt to pastoral poetry (see *pastoral drama* above).

A romantic comedy which was a favorite of both Elizabethan and later audiences was Thomas Dekker's *The Shoemaker's Holiday* (1599), and, as it is representative of the genre, let us review what happens. Dekker's play opens with the London Lord Mayor, Sir Roger Otley, talking about his daughter Rose in conjunction with Lincoln's nephew Lacy. Both are against a marriage between their children, and this of course represents an *obstacle to love* (the conventional problem of a romantic comedy and, we should remember, one of the features of earlier comedy). Shortly, the audience is introduced to the mad shoemaker of Tower Street, Simon Eyre, his prattling wife, and his lusty helpers. One of his workers, Rafe, newly married to Jane, has been drafted to fight against the French. Lacy, meanwhile, decides to disguise himself as a Dutch shoemaker, Hans, and goes to work for Simon Eyre. The Lord Mayor, in the meantime, decides that he would like his daughter Rose to marry Hammon, but she refuses because she still loves Lacy. Hammon pleads a romance to Jane and convinces her that Rafe is dead (again, this is very typical of romantic comedy: introducing confusion as to who is alive, and in what condition), although in fact Rafe has returned wounded. When Hammon's servant takes a shoe to be used in preparing the wedding shoes for Jane to Rafe, Rafe recognizes the shoe and thus prepares to go to the wedding.

In the meantime, Simon becomes first the Sheriff and then the new Lord Mayor of London. He agrees to help Lacy and Rose marry secretly, as well as to help Rafe prevent Jane from marrying Hammon. In the end, Lincoln and Sir Roger Otley go to St. Faith's Church to prevent their children from marrying, only to find that this is where Hammon is trying, futilely, to marry Jane! Dodger, Lincoln's servant who has been searching for Lacy, reports that Lacy has married Rose after all. The King is called in and makes everyone happy. He pacifies the angry parents by divorcing Rose and Lacy—only to turn right around and remarry them! He extends favors to Simon Eyre and the other shoemakers and all ends happily. Jane agrees to stay with her husband Rafe.

As is suggested by this brief plot summary, the play is light, spirited, entertaining, and, of course, all about love. The source of Dekker's play was a series of prose tales about romantic shoemakers (Thomas Deloney's *The Gentle Craft*). The dialogue of Simon and his fellow workers is delightful (and similar, really, to the playful bantering of Bottom and his company of actors in *A Midsummer Night's Dream*). Dekker's play is an excellent comedy and, in fact, easily rivaled Shakespeare's comedies which were playing at the other theater. Love, and the search for happy solutions to lovers' complications, provides the main motive behind the action. Furthermore, there is a characteristic democratic atmosphere, mixing up and involving all levels of society from shoemaker to king. The ending is happy and easily engineered (recall the simplistic resolution at the end of Peele's *Arraignment of Paris* discussed in *pastoral drama,* p. 137). It is quite typical of romantic comedies to have the various representatives of different social levels come together in the end of the play for a feast (for example, the ending of *A Midsummer Night's Dream*).

In romantic comedy the main goal becomes the happy resolution of problems. Shakespeare's *The Two Gentlemen of Verona* is a good case in point; it is a refreshing romantic comedy with a very simple story which is uncomplicated by any secondary plot. Some critics have observed that in this play, as in some of Shakespeare's other early comedies such as *Love's Labor's Lost* and *A Midsummer Night's Dream,* there are numerous touches of irony which seem to suggest that Shakespeare was poking fun at the conventions of romantic love while at the same time relying on them for the development of the action of his play. In any case, the play exhibits all of the characteristics of romantic comedy—love problems, considerable action taking place in a forest, the idea of banishment, the idea of fickleness in love (one character is named Proteus—the mythical sea god able to change to different forms—to represent fickleness), and the pastoral motif of the debate over the quality of life in town (court) versus that of life in the forest. In lines suggestive of many in *As You Like It,* in this earlier play we find Valentine coming to prefer life in the woods to his previous life in the town:

> How use doth breed a habit in a man!
> This shadowy desert, unfrequented woods,
> I better brook than flourishing people towns.

In the end of the play we find a typical element of romantic comedy as the fickle lover, Proteus, admits his silliness; Julia announces who she really is and explains that it is better for women to change their shape than for men to change their minds. Proteus must admit openly that fickleness in love creates all kinds of trouble. All the outlaws are pardoned, and, as at the end of *The Shoemaker's Holiday,* a marriage and a feast are announced. Romantic comedy, then, leads to pleasant feelings while at the same time it makes fun of the problems which arise from the foolishness of people in love—but always with the delightful corollary suggestion that none of us would want it any other way!

Comedy of Manners

This term defines the comedies of the Restoration which were pointedly satirical and which mocked, with considerable *wit* and sophistication, the mores of highly cultured, "proper" society. That is, the *manners* and the fashions of the upper social class were rendered laughable. The comedy of manners flourished in the Restoration period and was best attempted by William Congreve (1670–1729) in his *The Way of the World.* Deriving from Jonsonian "comedy of humors," Congreve's characters have dominant traits (suggested by names such as Fainall and Marwood—who would mar the happy ending). A particular societal group, with all its snobberies and pettiness, becomes the target of the antagonist Mirabell, who is anxious to expose the group's viciousness and absurdity. The twin comic subjects of money and joy are humorously put into a societal context. Later, the genre was also successfully attempted by Oliver Goldsmith (1728–1774) in *She Stoops to Conquer* (see *mistaken identity,* pp. 112, 124) and Richard Sheridan (1751–1826) in *The Rivals.*

In a comedy of manners, the characters are generally *types,* the plot unusually elaborate, and the action is subordinated to satire. "Wit-combats" abound and become the main repartee of the play. Jealous husbands, fops, malcontents, and other character types are attacked ("gulled") with witty satire. The intention of comedy of manners is, as Pope said of satire, to heal with morals what it hurts with wit. One of the interesting conventions of comedy of manners is what is usually referred to as the "love game," a kind of running debate or duel between a pair of "sophisticated" immoral lovers. The strongest features of comedy of manners, in any case, are sharp satire and plots designed to allow one character to "outwit" another. And the French comedy of manners written by Molière has given us our best examples of satire which is as meaningful as it is entertaining. Richard Wilbur's English translation of Molière's French *Le Misanthrope* has been delighting American audiences for several years. The witty fashioning of the rhymed couplets, the hilarious thrusts against the foolishness of certain kinds of characters—particularly the grumbling titular character, the gossiping lady, and the love-sick young poet. Dramatists who have written comedies of manners—Sheridan, Goldsmith, Wilde, Coward, and others—have, for the most part, consciously decided to use satire rather than romance as the mainspring of their plays. (Most comedies are, fundamentally, either romantic *or* satiric.) In the typical plot of a comedy of manners there is complexity of structure but not of idea. Incidents are compounded almost *ad infinitum*, and, as some critics have suggested, "society" virtually becomes the hero, while the other characters become submerged in the witty ins and outs of "one-up-manship." The humorous exposure of vanity, pettiness, and affectation tends to make the audience more tolerant of human foibles.

Sentimental Comedy

As comedy of manners developed as a reaction to Puritan sternness, sentimental comedy developed as a reaction to comedy of manners. Thus sentimental comedy is sometimes described as "reformed comedy." The English essayist and dramatist Richard Steele (1672–1729) was the main force behind the rise of sentimental comedy, and his *The Conscious Lovers* (1722) is generally considered the best example of the genre. Sentimental comedy is overtly didactic and places "message" above dramatic impact. Sentimental comedy, furthermore, has a certain parallel to bourgeois tragedy because it takes middle-class people for its principal characters and attempts to render their attitudes and feelings in a very emotional (sentimental) way. Let us consider what happens in Steele's *The Conscious Lovers*.

Steele's *The Conscious Lovers* is similar to Goldsmith's *She Stoops to Conquer*. At the center of the play is a mistaken identity. The plot, in brief, is that Sir John Bevil's young son John Bevil is about to be married to Mr. Sealand's daughter Lucinda, even though he is not in love with her and even though she is in love with his friend Myrtle. John, in fact, loves Indiana, a girl he has taken care of ever since her father had, presumably, died. In the end it turns out that John *can* marry Indiana, because she is *also* the daughter of Mr. Sealand, her lost father. Lucinda is thus free to marry Myrtle, while Cimberton, a pompous cousin who has been hoping for a marriage into an estate, is made to leave (besides, now that another daughter has been discovered the estate would be halved and this would not have been enough for him anyway).

In the course of the play we also find the humorous development of the romance between a servant, Tom, and a maid, Phillis; the contrast between their simple, uncomplicated love and the entangled marital "arrangements" attempted by upper middle-class families underlines what Steele sees as the folly and vanity of the latter.

There is a great deal of humor throughout the play, as, for example, when Tom and Myrtle disguise themselves as a pair of family lawyers, or when Myrtle disguises himself as a rich uncle of Cimberton. (These disguises tend to reinforce the humor arising from the basic unknown—or mixed—identity at the center of the play, namely, that Indiana is also Mr. Sealand's daughter.)

The world of sentimental comedy is that of comfortable upper middle-class eighteenth-century England with its addiction for social virtues and proper marriages. Sincerity replaces satire; the audience is sincerely moved, for example, by young Bevil's earnest love for Indiana and his rebellion against being asked to marry someone else. *The Conscious Lovers* shows the marked concern for gentility and middle-class respectability which were so characteristic of the genre. There is no cynical quality, nor doubt about the young lovers; young Bevil is upright, and thus admirable. That love has to do with marriage and not with marriage *settlements* underlines the middle-class sincerity of the genre.*

* It is interesting and significant to notice, finally, that Edward Moore (Fielding's friend), who wrote the best mid-eighteenth-century sentimental comedy, *The Foundling* (1748), also wrote one of the best bourgeois tragedies, *The Gamester* (1753).

Melodrama

Though originally a *melodrama* was a kind of Greek play containing numerous songs, it now simply designates the kind of play in which the characters tend to represent absolutes, and, particularly, good and evil (or virtue and vice). In melodrama, which was particularly popular in the nineteenth century (and led also to much of the "vaudeville" of the American stage), virtue is almost always victorious over vice, though the dramatist attempts to introduce as much suspense as possible. Artistically speaking, we can openly recognize that melodrama does not have too much to offer. It is often improbable, often a kind of boring tragedy (or, as some critics express it, *tragedy manqué*), and the characters are apt to become extreme stereotypes. Nevertheless, melodrama endured because the public wanted it to, and as a dramatic kind of entertainment, it still deserves consideration.

Late Nineteenth-Century Experimenting

During the course of the later nineteenth century, many of the standard genres began to dissolve into a curious melting pot. Playwrights seemed to regard their plays as *individual dramas* of various kinds. We can suggest the scope of the experimentation simply by considering some of the subtitles of the plays of George Bernard Shaw (1856–1950): *The Philanderer* (1893) was "A Topical Comedy"; *Arms and the Man* (1894), "An Anti-Romantic Comedy"; *Candida* (1894), "A Mystery"; *The Man of Destiny* (1895), "A Fictitious Paragraph of History"; *Man and Superman* (1901–1903), "A Comedy and Philosophy"; *The Shewing-Up of Blanco Posnet* (1909), "A Sermon in Crude Melodrama"; *Heartbreak House* (1913–1916), "A Fantasia in the Russian Manner on English Themes"—and so forth.

Shaw shared in the nineteenth-century techniques of melodrama and often relied on some of the conventional melodramatic characters (hero, heroine, clergyman, deserted orphan, villain, etc.), but his plays, as highly individualized creations, quickly surpassed the conventionality of basic genre. Let us briefly consider what happens in his popular "Mystery," *Candida.*

In *Candida,* which is often considered Shaw's most expertly constructed play, Shaw presents the "triangle" love story, but he makes it the basis for a highly intriguing and subtle play. There is a husband, the forty-year-old Christian Socialist clergyman James Morell, his thirty-three-year-old wife, Candida, and the shy, eighteen-year-old poet-protagonist, Eugene Marchbanks. The outline of the story is simple enough: Morell befriends and brings home Marchbanks who in turn falls in love with Candida. Morell slowly becomes enraged as it becomes clear that the young poet seriously desires to replace him as Candida's husband. When Candida is forced to choose between them, she is loyal to the weaker man, her husband. Candida has long been aware of her husband's lack of perception about her feelings and has been deeply moved by Marchbanks. Part of the "mystery" of the play is the reason that Marchbanks departs not as a disheartened or disappointed lover, but as a new, liberated man who is aware, at last, of his own powers.

Shaw's play is, then, a breaking away from the conventional "triangle" love melodrama. The wife does *not* leave her husband —as, say, Nora leaves Helmar in Ibsen's *A Doll's House*—and the marriage is *not* wrecked. The play does *not* become a domestic tragedy, but instead remains, as Shaw intended, a curious "mystery."

Realistic drama also represented the late nineteenth-century and early twentieth-century attempts to depart, in varying degree, from some of the restricting forces of the specific genres. In a *realistic* play we find an effort to focus on the most ordinary citizens of the world—shopkeepers, bankers, middle-class working people, and so forth—and on their common, understandable varieties of living and suffering. The main goal is authenticity, or the breaking down of any felt differences between art and life. The characters talk in straightforward, unembellished prose. They are involved not simply in unheroic events, but instead in completely common ones.

Realism was not actually a *new* force in drama. The extreme emphasis on it, however, was new, and in the late nineteenth century realism, rather than, say, comedy or tragedy, became a goal in itself. A kind of nongeneric quality was being elevated over specific genres. Shaw, Ibsen, and Chekhov all tried to draw increased attention, in a realistic manner, to the pressures and forces of middle-class society. Chekhov's *The Cherry Orchard* (1903–1904) represents the culminating drive of realism in his plays. He thought of it as a comedy, and in some ways it is. But it becomes something more than that because of the extreme efforts at realism. Let us consider what happens in this play.

A Russian family, headed by Lyubov Ranevskaya and her brother Gayev, is locked in the inertia which characterized many of the well-to-do upper class following the rise of the peasants. Unable to accept the disappearance of the master-peasant relationship, the family lives in the country and dwindles away its financial assets. Lopahin, a rising merchant, acquires through auction the family's entire estate which includes a beautiful cherry orchard. Chekhov focuses sharply on the very human inability of this formerly well-to-do family to accept the change which the events of Russian history have wrought. Gayev himself, when faced with the disaster, simply mutters about his pool game—"eight ball in the side pocket," and so forth.

Chekhov's family-in-decline can be seen both as comic and as pathetic. The members of the Russian family refuse to deal realistically with their situation. This understandable human failure becomes a sharply focused form of *realism*. That is to say, the characters become real, because they are all dreamers, and the massive irony of this situation overwhelms the audience. The play is a *comedy*, because Gayev and his family have a *ludicrous* inability to accept change. They could have had their cherry orchard cut down, leased their land, and allowed it to become "developed" as a group of small lots. Unable to accept this idea, however, and viewing the orchard as symbolic of the beauty and splendor to which they were formerly entitled, their entire estate is sold at auction while they retreat unrealistically into a home dance. As the play progresses toward Lopahin's victory, Anya, Lybov Ranevskaya's seventeen-year-old daughter, and Varya, her twenty-two-year-old adopted daughter, join with the others in refusing to admit or prevent the final horror of the loss of their home, prestige, and way of life. The final dispossession is a "just" reward to this family unable to accept reality, but it is also tragic and generates pity. The *realism* of the play, however, dominates such generic considerations. The pettiness of the behavior of a family faced with ruin is completely understandable, because each of us in the audience knows how hard it is to be realistic, particularly in the face of impending crisis or adversity. The characters constantly talk in a way which seems real to us, and with them we pass from reality to illusion. Consider, for example, the following dialogue:

MME. RANEVSKAYA. What should we do? Tell us what to do!

LOPAHIN. I've been telling you every day. Every day I keep saying the same thing! The cherry orchard and the land must be leased for summer cottages and it must be done very soon, now. The auction is on your very doorstep! Do try to understand! Once you decide definitely on the summer cottages, then you will be given as much money as you like and you'll be saved.

MME. RANEVSKAYA. The summer cottages and the tenants! Excuse me, but it sounds so trivial.

GAYEV. I agree with you completely.

LOPAHIN. Either I shall burst out crying or start screaming or faint dead away! I can't stand it! You absolutely exhaust me! (*to Gayev*) And you're an old woman!

GAYEV. What?

LOPAHIN. An old woman! (*He starts to leave.*)

MME. RANEVSKAYA (*frightful*). No, don't go. Stay, dear friend. I beg you. Perhaps we'll think of something!

LOPAHIN. Think of what?

MME. RANEVSKAYA. Don't leave, I beg you. With you here, it's somehow more cheerful. (*pause*) I expect something dreadful to happen, as if the house were about to crash down on us.

GAYEV (*in deep thought*). Double into the corner pocket . . . bank shot in the side.

MME. RANEVSKAYA. We have greatly sinned . . .

LOPAHIN. What sins could you possibly have committed?

GAYEV (*putting candy in his mouth*). They say I've eaten up an entire fortune in candy!

In this kind of conversation, Chekhov presents characters shuffling back and forth from reality to illusion, and in their pathetic vascillation we discover the more profound realism.

An understandable turning from *realism* to *naturalism* also took place in the late nineteenth century. While realism tries to present people as they are, in an almost simplistic way, naturalism tries to go further by suggesting the *reasons why people are as they are.* Naturalism, then, is based on ancestral influences, environmental forces, and psychological development. The Swedish dramatist August Strindberg (1849–1912) referred to his play *Miss Julie* (1888) as the "Swedish drama's first *naturalistic* tragedy." And just as realism supplants generic considerations in a play like Chekhov's *The Cherry Orchard,* so too the "tragedy" of *Miss Julie* is subordinated to the larger idea of naturalism. The characters' motives are viewed as complicated, because they develop from hereditary, environmental, and psychological forces, rather than simply from the circumstances or course of the dramatic action per se.

The story of *Miss Julie,* like that of Shaw's *Candida,* is simple. But while Shaw's play ends with a mystery, Strindberg's ends with a suicide. The thirty-year-old valet, Jean, seduces his master's daughter, the twenty-five-year-old title character. The seduction leads Julie, for a complexity of reasons, to kill herself. Strindberg pictures her suicide, however, not as a distraught result of seduction, but rather as the horrible and virtually inevitable culmination of environmental and psychological necessity—which is further conditioned by the clash of classes represented by the seduction of a woman higher in society by a man who is lower.

When we think, then, of Ibsen's *A Doll's House* in which the wife leaves her husband, of Shaw's *Candida* in which the wife stays with a weak husband, and of Strindberg's *Miss Julie* in which the seduced girl kills herself, we sense a new commitment to individualistic expressions of ordinary problems, and genre seems to be in a lesser position relative to larger, abstract, organizing ideas like realism and naturalism.

Another form of late nineteenth-century experimentation in the drama is discovered in the plays of William Butler Yeats

(1865–1939) who avoided realism and instead concentrated on *poetic* content and the potential energy of drama. The realism of Ibsen and Chekhov and the naturalism of Strindberg did not, somehow, take the audience far enough. Life, Yeats thought, needed to be enlarged upon, needed to be transformed—at least in part—into myth, and this transformation could take place through the introduction into drama of an intensely poetic vision and language. Yeats' *On Baile's Strand* (1903) is not simply "a tragedy," but instead, as Yeats termed it, "Greek Tragedy, spoken with a Dublin accent." In Yeats' experimenting, as in that of Shaw, Chekhov, Ibsen, Strindberg, and others, we discover, then, the steady erosion of traditional generic drama, and this erosion led almost inevitably to twentieth-century "experimental plays."

Experimental Plays: Modern Drama

Over the centuries, a great deal of drama has been considered, by contemporaries, *avant garde*. After all, every dramatist tries to do new things, but some, of course, try harder than others. The experiments of the dramatists at the turn of the last century were catalytic forces to an even greater "shake-up" of generic distinctions, and the result was that much of the drama of this century has indeed been "experimental" to an unusual degree.

The audience is virtually bombarded by experiment, for example, in Bertold Brecht's (1898–1956) *The Good Woman of Setzuan* in which there are both strange songs presented stage front as interruptions and large projected signs flashing various ludicrous messages over the heads of the actors. The third act of Tom Stoppard's recent success, *Rosencrantz and Guildenstern Are Dead* (1967), opens in complete darkness and soft sea sounds. The seemingly insane dialogue becomes exciting in the darkness. Brecht's *Galileo*, first translated into English in the late 1930s, is an experimental tragicomedy which alternates heroic and unheroic qualities and actions in a bizarre manner.

Perhaps the keynote to the experimentalism of modern drama, as distinct from earlier experimentation, is the elevation of the *idea* of experimentalism. That is, experimental qualities are self-consciously and artistically pursued as ends in themselves, and thus a new theory of dramatic construction arises.

Most critics now use the term "experimental drama" to describe—in an admitted oversimplification—those plays which, in their self-conscious flexibility, depend neither on conventional genres nor on the larger principles of realism and naturalism. Stated in this way, experimental drama becomes a large net into which fall seemingly unlimited varieties of experimentation represented by such types as *psychodrama, drama of the absurd, expressionistic drama, happenings,* and *living theater.*

Luigi Pirandello's (1867–1936) *Six Characters in Search of an Author* (1921) is, as the title suggests, a deliberate experiment. It is a curious play which becomes a play both about itself and about drama in general. The six characters come to the manager of a theater and explain that they were created by an author who did not afterward desire to make a drama of his own creations. The characters are thus now "in search of an author." The manager, who is in the process of staging another play (also, humorously, by Pirandello!), interrupts his work to become the author for this about-to-be-created play. This is, of course, an imaginative reworking of the conventional device of the *play-within-the-play,* but it is also an experiment in chaos and in humorously depicting the twin processes of writing and producing a play. The chaos of producing a written play is transformed into the chaos of producing an unwritten play, and thus the larger, single "play" demonstrates, as Pirandello's manager claims, the process of going out of the frying pan and into the fire. The experimentation of the play *becomes* a critical principle of dramatic composition, namely, that the characters a dramatist creates can easily and naturally proceed through actions which are inevitable outgrowths of their individual personalities. They do not need to be "manipulated," but rather simply observed. Pirandello is asserting that when characters are born, they acquire an independence which transcends the idea that they are but "roles"; the characters can do things which the author, in first creating them, did not conceive of. (They even can, for example, go out and search for another author.)

The conflicts which develop between the characters and the manager and his workers (property man, prompter, machinist, secretary, door-keeper, scene-shifters, and other extras), generate a humorous and sympathetic understanding of playwrighting, a "critical" sense of what some of the pitfalls of playwrighting are (attempting to moralize too much, for example), and pinpoints some of the unfortunate gaps between the written play ("the book") and the play as it is performed on the stage. Humor and critical theory merge as it becomes steadily apparent that the manager and the actors are unable to create a play, because they cannot agree as to what a play should be (Pirandello asks, for example, whether there should be more action or more philosophizing).

At the end of the play, the actors have a little girl drown and a boy die. Maybe it is "pretense" and maybe it is "reality." The distinction underscores the entire experimentation of the play which the manager brings to a close by saying, "Pretense? Reality? To hell with it all! Never in my life has such a thing happened to me. I've lost a whole day over these people, a whole day!"

Six Characters in Search of an Author underscores all distinctions with which drama inevitably deals, but particularly with that between reality and illusion. Stated more emphatically, by using a play-within-the-play in a new, experimental way, Pirandello is able to combine art and life in an extraordinary, exciting manner. The precise nature of artistic reality is illusive—and this idea is behind the bulk of modern experimental drama.

A Note on Other Kinds of Plays

It is now to be hoped that the student has a good understanding of the basic characteristics of tragedy and comedy as they were written in ancient Greece, and of the most significant kinds of tragedy and comedy which have evolved since then. We have looked at a few kinds of plays which are not properly comedy or tragedy (such as heroic drama, chronicle play, pastoral drama, melodrama, and experimental drama), and the student should be aware that there are other genres of lesser importance and interest which we do not have time to discuss in this book. Nevertheless, a few of them can be named here.

The *masque* is a kind of courtly entertainment (recall our comments about *interludes*) in which the main characters (*masquers*) enter, having just traveled from a distant land, recite some accounts of deeds past and sing a few songs, ask the ladies at the court to dance with them, and then depart. Another minor kind of drama is known as the *mime,* a type of popular comedy developed in fifth-century Italy in which the daily events of men's lives were portrayed through dancing, gesture, and humorous dialogue. Mimes eventually became overly sensual in their focus and were thus attacked by the church. However, the mime is often credited for certain dimensions of the humor we still find in comedy (and in much vaudeville). *Closet drama* designates drama intended to be *read* rather than performed on the stage. Byron's nineteenth-century *Manfred,* for example, was probably meant to be a closet drama, though in recent years it has been given successful production (the poet Donald Hall played the title character in an excellent production in 1968 by the Lord Chamberlain's Players at the University of Michigan). Fielding's *Tom Thumb the Great* (successfully staged by the Lord Chamberlain's Players in 1969), a drama which was designed as a burlesque of heroic drama, is more *literary* than dramatic. Milton said that his *Samson Agonistes* was intended to be read, not performed. One fairly important kind of play is known as the *Tragedy of Blood.* This is an intensified, *more* sensational version of *Senecan drama* in general and of *revenge tragedy* in particular (Kyd's *A Spanish Tragedy* represents all three kinds of plays, and students should refer to the discussion of it in the section on *Senecan and Elizabethan drama,* p. 127). I do not mean to be opening up a grab-bag of genres with these final remarks. Important and lasting genres like *romantic tragedy* and *comedy of manners* are the student's main concern. But other kinds of plays do exist, and together they suggest the final plasticity of dramatic composition. Because drama has as its purpose, as Hamlet directed the players within his play, to hold up a mirror to nature *and the age,* it is alive and always changing.

PART THREE

Fiction

What Is Fiction?

To a certain extent, the term "fiction," which designates that class of literature comprising works of *imaginative prose narration,* is a misnomer because it carries connotations of falsehood. Basically, fiction is *story-telling,* but the province of fiction includes reality. Fiction asserts ideas about certain themes or subjects—the struggle between man and nature, for example—and while the story may be "made-up" or imagined, the truth is not. Some novelists, in fact, have complained that the world, with its complex reality, is more imaginative and stimulating than anything that they might invent. Edmund Burke wrote: "Fiction lags after truth, invention is unfruitful, and imagination cold and barren." Obviously his statement is an extreme one, but it does constructively suggest that fiction follows reality and is dependent on it to a great extent. Indeed, fiction tries to suggest ideas in a more discernible and meaningful fashion than reality, and this was the idea which the nineteenth-century novelist William Thackeray probably had in mind when he wrote, "Fiction carries a greater amount of truth in solution than the volume which purports to be all true."

A *narrative* is the story of events or experiences, and narrative fiction is a story told in prose. Someone, that is, is narrating (telling) the story which may be true or fictitious, and thus when we talk about fiction, we are talking about those stories which are invented—though they often could have happened. The whole line between fiction and reality has been challenged with increasing vigor in this century. Truman Capote's best-selling *In Cold Blood* was what he thought of as a "nonfiction novel" because it told the *true story* of a horrible murder, and yet in the telling, relied on all of the artistic devices of plot, characterization, and setting which writers telling fictitious stories generally use. Some writers, furthermore, have argued that life, after all, does not really contain many different stories—falling in love, the loss of innocence, tragic death, and so forth—and Willa Cather wrote that "There are only two or three human stories, and they go on repeating themselves as fiercely as if they had never happened before." Thus fiction takes as its province a reality which contains experiences which are repeated again and again, but never with any diminution of excitement for either participant or spectator. We might recall Keats' lines:

> Too many tears for lovers have been shed,
> Too many sighs give we to them in fee,
> Too much of pity after they are dead,
> Too many doleful stories do we see,
> Whose matter in bright gold were best be read;
>
> ("ISABELLA," lines 90–94)

The "doleful stories" of which Keats speaks will, of course, always be with us, as will other kinds of stories. Fiction, as a form of self-conscious invention, is one of man's oldest inheritances, and the momentum toward story-telling is secure.

Our approach to fiction must be a little different from our

approaches to poetry and to drama. The main reason is that fiction takes virtually unlimited forms. Rather than select certain distinctive forms, of which there are so many, for lengthy discussion, it seems better to think primarily in terms of the three conventional forms of fiction: *novel, novella,* and *short story.* All three forms are narrative prose. A novel is fictitious prose narrative of considerable length and generally has a fairly large number of incidents, as well as both major and minor characters; a *novella* is simply a short novel (the term *novella,* comes from the Italian phrase *novella narratio,* meaning new kind of story); a *short story* is generally less than 10,000 words in length.

There are some kinds of novels which have identifiable properties. The *picaresque novel* presents the various adventures of a rogue (*Moll Flanders*). The *romance* presents its story in a partly improbable setting; that is, a romance alters life a little in order to make a particular truth or idea more accessible to our imagination and understanding (*The Blithesdale Romance*). The *bildungsroman* is a "novel of education" in which the hero, a young man, is educated to the ways of the world; usually the *bildungsroman,* then, is about the human maturation process and about the *initiation* of youth into adult experiences (*David Copperfield*). A *psychological novel* contains, as the phrase suggests, considerable cerebration, and presents much of the narration through the inner workings of the characters' minds (*Crime and Punishment*). We also have the *stream-of-consciousness* novel, a psychological novel which is told through the mental wanderings of a single character (*The Red Badge of Courage*). There are numerous other kinds of novels, far too many to summarize here, and many which have yet to be written. John Barth (*Giles Goat Boy*) is experimenting with the entire art of novel writing in new and exciting ways, and Marshall McLuhan has warned us about setting limits for media.

The point is that fiction, unlike poetry and drama, is less dependent on form and style, because it can do virtually *anything.* This is not to suggest that form is unimportant in fiction (or *all*-important in poetry and drama), but rather that it makes more sense for us to consider the art of writing fiction in broader terms. Two *pastoral elegies* have a great deal in common, because of the *necessary* conventions of that poetic genre. It is important, therefore, to know those conventions. Two *romances,* on the other hand, may not have anything in common other than their improbability. Granted, some kinds of novels have particular conventions, but they are not as adamantly adhered to as are many of the conventions of poetry and drama. Finally, a student in a college literature course is not generally asked to *write* about fiction in the same manner in which he is asked to write about poetry. A professor rarely asks a student to "analyze a novel," though he frequently asks him to analyze a poem. Instead, the student is usually asked to write about a *particular aspect* of a novel—the nature of the characters, the development of the plot, the symbolism, the establishing of setting, the point of view, the style of narration, and so forth—and, because this book is intended to aid the college *writer,* it seems sensible to focus on the broad aims and artistic dimensions which novels, novellas, and short stories of different kinds all have in common.

What Does Fiction Do?

As fiction is story-telling, it is clear that it presents an account, told from a particular point of view (see *point of view,* p. 160), of various *incidents.* The incidents, taken together, form the *plot* and suggest the method of development. Sometimes all of the incidents do not bear directly on the plot, and sometimes they do. Thus when writing about the story-telling art of fiction, the student should consider which of the incidents are essential to the development (advancement) of the actual story. Sometimes certain incidents form a discernible *subplot,* which in turn is subordinated to the *main plot.* Some incidents introduce emotional intensity and others introduce comic relief; each incident, in other words, has a function similar to an individual scene in a play.

Episodic fiction, such as Dickens' early work, relies to a great extent on the piling up of countless incidents. Some novels place a greater balance on *characterization* than on incident. (There are various methods of characterization—action, dialogue, and description—and we will consider some of them in the next section.) At this point we are only trying to suggest clearly what happens in fiction: characters interact in a series of incidents. Furthermore, their interaction takes place within a particular *setting*. The setting of fiction—presented through literal and figurative descriptions, social attitudes, time, location, etc.—is extremely important and subject to tremendous artistic variation.

Particular works of fiction have particular qualities. There may be humor in one novel, moral purpose in a second, both in a third, and neither in a fourth. The student writing about a work of fiction has as his constant purpose the recording of its special qualities and its peculiarities of style. Also, fiction has a *raison d'être*. A novel may have been written to entertain a certain reading public which the author has clearly in mind (the white, educated, upper middle-class readers of *The New Yorker*, for example, who are steadily entertained by fiction writers like John Cheever and John Updike). A work of fiction may be written to suggest or assert a particular philosophy: we are all aware of the purpose behind Aldous Huxley's *Brave New World*. Fiction is exciting, because writers of fiction have diversified reasons for writing. James Baldwin has written from a very personal point of view in his novels, because he believes that one can really *only* write about one's own experiences. John Updike wrote his exploration of modern marital infidelity, *Couples*, both to entertain and to sound a danger signal. Philip Roth exploded the "Jewish mother" joke in *Portnoy's Complaint*. Norman Mailer is being considered by many critics less as a novelist than a kind of cultural phenomenon who also happens to write. Some fiction is written in order to philosophize, and some is written in order to entertain (and I do not want to suggest any definite division between the two, for most novels are written for both purposes, though with shades of emphasis). Nevertheless, each work of fiction is distinctive in terms of style, purpose, character, incident, setting, and theme. Sometimes we are conscious of the author's opinions and sometimes we are not. It is safe to say, in any case, that a fiction writer wants his work to have a particular *effect* on his readers, and in order to secure that effect, he manipulates artistically all of the elements of fiction—to which we now turn.

What Makes Fiction Art?

By the middle of the eighteenth century in England, prose fiction was established as a viable *art form.* Various simplistic tales and adventure stories had now been supplanted by a more glorious idea—the novel. Three of the writers responsible for the new artistic development of the novel were Samuel Richardson, Henry Fielding, and Tobias Smollett. Richardson (1689–1761) introduced greater psychological interest into fiction; Fielding (1707–1754), a greater sense of structure; and Smollett (1721–1771), more humor and burlesque. All three of these novelists were moralists, though in different ways, and all of them were artists with a deep interest in developing the as yet unknown capacities of prose fiction.

Daniel Defoe had written journalistic novels like *Moll Flanders,* but this kind of novel would prove only a poor relation of what the others were striving for. Defoe simply strung together innumerable incidents, and though this stringing process was not without its artistic dimension, it simply was too one-dimensional. Samuel Richardson was interested in the inner workings of the human mind, and his characters were therefore excellent psychological studies. He liked, in particular, to show the frustrating indecision behind much human thought. Richardson used what we call *the epistolary method,* the writing of letters to tell a story. Different characters all are able to make their *point of view* (see p. 160) known, because series of their individually composed letters are sent back and forth. Two characters will sometimes be found relating the same incident, but, because of their different attitudes, their accounts differ, and in the difference is a wealth of psychological study. We do not have time, here, to go into the enormous number of critical debates surrounding Richardson's masterpiece, *Clarissa*. Let us simply note that the success of this novel led to a host of other "epistolary" novels and enlarged the reading public's awareness of the *artistry* behind *point of view* in prose fiction.

Fielding wanted to show the way in which virtue works for the good of a man, and to do so he used humor and carefully contrived structural patterns in writing *Joseph Andrews* and *Tom Jones*. In both of these novels Fielding provided critical, explanatory introductions, and students interested in his art should read them carefully. Let us note here, however, that in the preface to *Joseph Andrews*, which critics take as the more important preface, Fielding talked about the *novel* as a "comic epic poem in prose." He knew that the epic had been given considerable critical discussion, and that his readers probably knew that an epic moved toward a specific goal, with each incident contributing to that movement. Fielding believed that episodes of fiction should work in the same way, and thus *Tom Jones* became one of the best *structured* works of fiction in the history of English literature. Fielding's artistic relating and interweaving of smaller and larger episodes is exciting and thorough. The reader feels that he is actually being brought into Fielding's world. Fielding's introduction of epic style and structure into fiction allowed other novelists to take up the genre with more ease.

Tobias Smollett introduced artistic concern for the smallest details of human nature. He also concentrated on telling his story (that is, he was less concerned for the precise structuring of episodes and more concerned with simply saying what he wanted to). Smollett explained *his* idea of the novel (all three of these early novelists were vitally concerned with defining their genre) in his preface to *Ferdinand Count Fathom*:

> A novel is a large diffused picture, comprehending the characters of life, disposed in different groups, and exhibited in various attitudes, for the purposes of a uniform plan, and general occurrence, to which every individual figure is subservient. But this plan cannot be executed with propriety, probability, or success, without a principal personage to attract the attention, unite the incidents, unwind the clue of the labyrinth, and at last close the scene by virtue of his own importance.

This focus on a single, principal character led to that kind of novel which follows, in the main, the adventures of a title character through the world at large (for example, Smollett's *Roderick Random*). Smollett's best experiment in the novel form, *Humphrey Clinker* (1771), was clearly in this pattern.

The growth of the English novel is a subject for another book—and, indeed, there are several good books available. I simply want to suggest, in this brief introduction, some of the *artistic* activity taking place as the novel, as we now think of it, began to take shape in the eighteenth century. From the beginning there was evident a sincere concern for telling a story in more than a direct way; *art* was needed to fashion characters, formulate the plot, make the world of the action immediate, and so forth. The student who wants to write about fiction should have a basic awareness of the craftsman's concern for his craft. Writing fiction is not like writing exposition or journalism; it is more self-consciously artistic. Writers want to produce clearly conceived *effects*.

Point of View

An author of prose fiction usually tries to achieve a certain "aesthetic distance" from his story, and he generally accomplishes this through the method of telling his story from a particular point of view. We can always identify the *narrator* (but not the author) of the story. Often a story is told by a narrator speaking in the *first person*. Consider the opening of Hemingway's *The Sun Also Rises;* the *I* is, throughout the novel, the voice of the major character, Jake:

> Robert Cohn was once middleweight boxing champion of Princeton. Do not think that I am very much impressed by that boxing title, but it meant a lot to Cohn. He cared nothing for boxing, in fact disliked it, but he learned it painfully and thoroughly to counteract the feeling of inferiority and shyness he had felt on being treated as a Jew at Princeton . . . In his last year at Princeton he read too much and took to wearing spectacles.

> I never met any one of his class who remembered him. They did not even remember that he was middleweight boxing champion.
>
> I mistrust all frank and simple people, especially when their stories hold together, and I always had a suspicion that perhaps Robert Cohn had never been middleweight boxing champion, and that perhaps a horse had stepped on his face, or that maybe his mother had been frightened or seen something as a young child, but I finally had somebody verify the story from Spider Kelly. Spider Kelly not only remembered Cohn. He had often wondered what had become of him.

In this fashion, Hemingway allows the reader to see that Jake (whose name we learn later), *as both a character and the narrator,* has a good view of things, has a grasp of the other characters —like Robert Cohn—and also a distinctive personality ("I mistrust all frank and simple people"). That the narrator is not impressed by Cohn's claim to have been the middleweight boxing champion at Princeton tells us as much about *him* as about Cohn. This method of telling the story from a *first-person I in the story* is very effective. John Knowles' *A Separate Peace* is designed in the same fashion. The book, in fact, opens with the word "I":

> I went back to the Devon School not long ago, and found it looking oddly newer than when I was a student there fifteen years before. It seemed more sedate than I remembered it, more perpendicular and strait-laced, with narrower windows and shinier woodwork, as though a coat of varnish had been put over everything for better preservation. But, of course, fifteen years before there had been a war going on.

We do not learn for quite some time that the narrator's name is Gene Forrester, but it is apparent from the beginning that the story is being told from his point of view and that he will be in it.

When a single voice is telling the whole story, and is aware of *everything,* he is referred to as an *omniscient narrator* (this is the pose taken by Thackeray in *Vanity Fair*) and has been used successfully by numerous great novelists.

An omniscient narrator imparts the feeling that he is simply taking the reader by the hand and "showing him around" in a particular world. Consider, for example, the opening of Anthony Trollope's *Doctor Thorne* (first published in London in 1858). The narrator is obviously omniscient:

> Before the reader is introduced to the modest country medical practitioner who is to be the chief personage of the following tale, it will be well that he should be made acquainted with some particulars as to the locality in which, and the neighbours among whom, our doctor followed his profession.

Notice the direct reference to "the reader"; this is the narrator's way of reminding his audience of the teacher-pupil, author-reader, or, almost, guide-tourist relationship which is about to begin. Notice the swift transition to "*our* doctor," a device of including the reader from this point on. This world is going to be completely available to the reader. And notice, too, that there is no "I" (though the voice of the narrator is clear and obviously all-knowing).

The narrator of *Tom Jones* is also omniscient. The voice tells us in the beginning that just as people who go into a restaurant like to look at the menu before spending any money, so too a reader ought to be given some idea of the "fare" (menu) which awaits him before committing himself to reading the book. The narrator then simply says:

> The provision, then, which we have here made is no other than *Human nature*. Nor do I fear that my sensible reader, though most luxurious in his taste, will start, cavil, or be offended, because I have named but one article . . . nor can the learned reader be ignorant, that in Human Nature, though here collected under one general name, is such a prodigious variety, that a cook will have sooner gone through all the several species of animal and vegetable food in the world, than an author will be able to exhaust so extensive a subject.

Fielding is establishing, at the outset, a distinct author-reader relationship. Fielding the author *becomes* Fielding the narrator. He will be the guide and take the reader through the vast realm of human nature; if the reader has any sense ("the *learned* reader cannot be ignorant"), he will see at once that this should be an enormous and fabulous journey! A few minutes later, Fielding returns to his restaurant-novel analogy by concluding:

> Having premised thus much, we will now detail those who like our bill of fare no longer from their diet, and shall proceed directly to serve up the first course of our history for their entertainment.

Notice that the "I" has become a "we"; the author is trying to *include* the reader from this point on—I am the keeper of the restaurant and chief cook; you are here to have a good meal; let us see what we *together* can do.

The omniscient narrator knows everything that has happened in the past, what is happening everywhere in the present, and, above all, what will happen later. This all-knowing quality is sometimes presented in the basic description of the setting, as, for example, the way in which the narrator of *Bleak House,* in the opening description of the law courts, shows his familiarity with the scene. This is on the second page of the book, and we hear the first-person omniscient narrator (*Bleak House* makes use of a *shifting* point of view; some chapters are narrated by an omniscient narrator and some are narrated in the form of a diary of a young girl, Esther):

> On such an afternoon, if ever the Lord High Chancellor ought to be sitting here—as here he is—with a foggy glory round his head, softly fenced in with crimson cloth and curtains, addressed by a large advocate with great whiskers, a little voice, and an interminable brief, and outwardly directing his contemplation to the lantern in the roof, where he can see nothing but fog. On such an afternoon, some score of members of the High Court of Chancery bar ought to be—as here they are—mistily engaged in one of the ten thousand stages of an endless cause, tripping one another up on slippery precedents, groping knee-deep in technicalities, running their goat-hair and horse-hair warded heads against walls of words, and making a pretence of equity with serious faces, as players might. On such an after-

> noon, the various solicitors in the cause, some two or three of whom have inherited it from their fathers, who made a fortune by it, ought to be—as are they not?—ranged in a line . . .

The mixture of *ought* and *is* becomes very effective through repetition, and allows us to sense the narrator's omniscience. He, we feel, is someone who has "been around," "knows the ropes," and will certainly be able to see this particular story in its full perspective.

Sometimes we discover what may be called, though imperfectly perhaps and only for purposes of discussion, a *selective omniscient narrator*—that is, a narrator who selects a particular character and knows everything about that character's thoughts but not very much about the thoughts of the other characters. Sometimes, too, this selective omniscience has a kind of omniscience manqué, or an *intentionally incomplete* understanding of a character. The narrator tells the reader he is not quite certain as to what a character's exact thoughts are, though he has, perhaps, a few ideas. Consider the way in which Henry James introduces Winterbourne, the young man in *Daisy Miller*:

> I hardly know whether it was the analogies or the differences that were uppermost in the mind of a young American who, two or three years ago, sat in the garden of the Trois Couronnes, looking about him, rather idly, at some of the graceful objects I have mentioned. It was a beautiful summer morning, and in whatever fashion the young American looked at things they must have seemed to him charming.

The *art* of this narration is very impressive. We have an authorial "I" relating the incidents and also *speculating* about his characters —this allies the author with the reader; we are all wondering *together* just what this young American is thinking, and while James *could* tell us—the character, after all, *is* his creation—he purposely decides *not* to be too definite, not to know everything, and thus is a kind of omniscient narrator manqué.

Thus we have the method of first-person narrator *in* the story (Jake talking in *The Sun Also Rises,* Nick Carroway in *The Great*

Gatsby, or Gene Forrester in A *Separate Peace*), omniscient narrator (the speaker in *Dr. Thorne* or *Tom Jones*), and incomplete omniscient narrators. At a greater "aesthetic distance," however, we have the direct, *third-person* point of view. In this method, the narrator tells the reader what is happening, but this narrator is *seeing* the story, and is *not in it*. The third-person point of view tends toward a great deal of description; we do not think that the narrator is *there*, only that he knows what is happening. This technique is well exemplified by the opening of a story, "Ivy Day in the Committee Room," from James Joyce's *The Dubliners*:

> Old Jack raked the cinders together with a piece of cardboard and spread them judiciously over the whitening dome of coals. When the dome was thinly covered his face lapsed into darkness but, as he set himself to fan the fire again, his crouching shadow ascended the opposite wall and his face slowly re-emerged into light. It was an old man's face, very bony and hairy. The moist blue eyes blinked at the fire and the moist mouth fell open at times, munching once or twice mechanically when it closed. When the cinders had caught he laid the piece of cardboard against the wall, sighed and said:
>
> "That's better now, Mr. O'Connor."
>
> Mr. O'Connor, a grey-haired young man, whose face was disfigured by many blotches and pimples, had just brought the tobacco for a cigarette into a shapely cylinder but when spoken to he undid his handiwork meditatively. Then he began to roll the tobacco again meditatively and after a moment's thought decided to lick the paper.

This kind of third-person narrative is perhaps the most common point of view we encounter in fiction. And often the nature of the narrator, the personality of the voice we hear, is part of the meaning of the story (particularly in "sophisticated" fiction). We generally need to think of author and narrator as two distinct *voices*, particularly, for example, in many of Hawthorne's stories where the *narrator* is as great an artistic *creation* as are the *characters* themselves. The best place to begin a study of a work of fiction, in any case, is with the voice, the point of view. This, after all, is obviously the narrator's first concern (he has to begin the book in some way, in some voice), and it should also be ours.

Plot

In our general discussion of *dramatic structure* we referred to Aristotle's dictum that plot is the soul of tragedy. To some literary critics plot is also the soul of fiction, and certainly plot is one thing which all fiction has in common. Plot is subject to considerable artistic manipulation, though there is usually a general commitment on the writer's part either to a plot resembling the *episodic nature of epic* or to one resembling the *climactic nature of drama.* A novelist relies on *episodes,* or *incidents,* to put together his book. There are almost infinite patterns of organization, though the greatest is still probably chronological. Laurence Sterne (1713–1768) in his rollicking, satirical novel *Tristram Shandy,* deliberately juggled his time scheme and even opened the novel, with great humor, at the moment *before* his actual conception (imagining his mother and father in bed, and his mother, in fact, interrupting his amorous father to ask him if he remembered to wind the clock!). Throughout the novel the time scheme is deliberately mixed up and thus serves as a burlesque of novels in which there is an orderly chronological progression with one incident following another with logical regularity and reliability. Richardson's *Clarissa* was essentially climactic, and modeled to a certain extent after the pattern of tragedy—with rising action, climax, and falling action. *Tom Jones,* as we have already suggested, was modeled after epic.

The student writing about fiction must study the relation of incidents to each other and, more importantly, to the whole of the book. Is there a *strongly unified whole?* Do all the incidents bear on the *main plot?* The structure of the plot is simply the pattern of the incidents. Usually there is some action which is at least partly unrelated to the main action. Whether or not a plot is of a specifically dramatic nature, the odds are that it is designed in such a way as to have a *climax* (though the climax may be located in different parts—early, middle, late). Let us consider the climax of John Knowles' brilliant short novel of prep school life in 1942, *A Separate Peace.* The narrator, Gene Forrester, and his best friend, Finny, have a competitive but nevertheless warm relationship. There are various episodes which deepen the rivalry between them and introduce various emotional patterns in the relationship between the two of them as well as in those between them and the rest of the boys in the group. Finny creates a series of war games in which all of the boys militantly compete. (Knowles is suggesting that it is impossible for the boys to enjoy a truly "separate peace" away from the world turmoil.) Finny falls from a tree while the boys are pretending to be diving into the water from a torpedoed ship during wartime. Gene is not sure whether he made the branch jiggle or whether Finny's fall was an accident. Gene is given a gruesome mock-trial by the other boys and when he is accused of causing Finny's fall, Finny runs out of the room and has a bad fall down the white marble stairs of the school building. The doctor who operates on Finny's leg allows air to get into the blood stream and thus Finny dies.

Knowles' structure has tremendous art in it. The first fall brings to a halt the first major section of the novel (and it is a short novel) and introduces a macabre kind of adult suspicion into the youthful, playful world.* Finny's tragedy also serves notice on the boys at Devon School that they are not exempt from disaster nor from the psychology of warfare which suffuses the times. Furthermore, the metaphor of "the fall" will be used throughout the book. The first fall leads to the "trial" of Gene, led by Brinker Hadley, the arch-militant student, and the trial in turn leads to cruelty; Finny's distress at hearing that his friend may have caused his fall from the tree leads to his second, fatal fall.

Knowles' plot is designed in such a way that things which happen early in the story connect very well to things which happen later; each incident (and there are many of them) relates to the overall progression of the story (which centers, generally,

* The novel is basically a psychological one, and as a meticulous study of adolescent feelings and problems is similar to Salinger's *Catcher in the Rye.*

around the nature of war and, specifically, around Finny's fall). The climax, Finny's fall from the tree, arrives early in the book (end of the fourth chapter, out of thirteen); there is lengthy *falling action*, as there might be in a play; we witness the steady deepening of the conflict, Gene's mental anxiety, and the final "catastrophe" of the novel, Finny's death.

Herman Melville's (1819–1891) *Moby Dick* centers around Ahab's violent, avenging pursuit of the great white whale. There are countless incidents which seem, at first, unconnected to this main plot. However, on further consideration, we realize that almost everything in the book depends on the reader's awareness of both the nature of whaling—the costliness, the danger, the complexity, the uncertainty, etc.—and the nature of the personalities of the crew pursuing this particular whale. The book is a *unified whole* and the various incidents all lead, in different ways and of course with different intensity, to the final confrontation between Ahab and Moby Dick. We do not find the picaresque tradition of having the hero go through a series of basic episodes, which we find in *Tom Jones* or *Don Quixote*, but we do find the same tight relating of parts to the whole. Every novel or story has a different *method of development*, in other words, but every novel must either have its incidents working toward a unified whole or else have some incidents working with independence. Generally, incidents are dramatically juxtaposed: an incident of emotional despair, for example, is perhaps followed by one of polite conversation or emotional relief. A good novelist advances different aspects of the plot simultaneously while always having his eye on the overall, or "organic," *plot*.

Characters

The characters of fiction are as varied and exciting as their real-life counterparts and many of them enter into the permanent landscape of our own world—Robert Louis Stevenson's Long John Silver, Dickens' David Copperfield, Swift's Gulliver, Tarkington's Penrod, and Joyce's Stephen Daedalus. Characters come to life in fiction and those who are developed with art and humanity often survive to dwell among us as friends, and sometimes even as intimate friends. Because characters are so different and dwell in particular worlds it is dangerous to overgeneralize about them. Nevertheless, there are certain basic considerations of characters which students should make, and these considerations can perhaps best be approached through the formation of general questions. For example, is a character *major* or *minor?* Is he stereotyped or distinctly individualistic? Is he supposed to be a *believable* member of the human race? Is he a "product of his age and his environment"? Does his behavior reflect on a place and moment in time? What is the psychological *motivation* behind his behavior? Is he presented *artistically?* The answers to these and similar questions form a basis from which we can arrive at the essential meaning of specific characters.

MAJOR AND MINOR. The distinction here is obvious enough and most of what we have said about characters in *plays* who are either *major* or *minor* can be applied to characters in fiction. A major character is generally present during a substantial portion of the book and is involved in the main plot. He is usually discussed (sometimes in the first person) at considerable length, and we attach importance to his actions and their consequences.

The number of major characters in a given work varies. A major character is inherently important, and we take a long, hard look at him in order to understand an author's meaning. Minor characters, who also vary in number, enter and depart from the action with considerable frequency, and while they are often entertaining or dramatic, they are less important to the total significance of the work. Minor characters are often outstanding, exciting, and entirely memorable (though I hesitate to name some of them for fear of omitting someone's favorites). Minor characters often serve as "links" between major characters, and they also are often extremely functional in terms of developing the plot. Minor characters are only infrequently presented with any sort of extensive psychological analysis. As the distinction between major characters and minor characters is relatively simple, it would be unduly academic to belabor it.

ROUND AND FLAT. When a character is presented as a complex individual with various personality features and distinctive expressions of being and is, further, shown to be a product of various behavioral forces which have, to some extent, determined his personality, he is said to be a *round character*. Generally speaking, round is synonymous with complex. When a character never becomes particularly complicated, we think of him, instead, as a *flat character*. *Stereotyped* villains, molls, rascals, and so forth are flat, while the youthful protagonists in "novels of initiation" are round. Melville's Ahab and Dostoevsky's Raskolnikov are round; Dickens' Gradgrind is flat. That a character is playing a thematic role (representing a particular abstract quality such as evil, lust, or greed) does not make him flat; rather, he is flat if he is simple and does not receive extensive psychological development.

Criterion of Credibility. One of the first and most important questions we need to ask about a character is whether or not he is credible (believable). Does he seem to be someone who might very plausibly exist in the real world, or does he seem primarily an imaginative creation (only partly human, perhaps) designed to fulfill particular functions in the fictional world of which he is a part? When we apply the criterion of credibility we are, really, doing two things. First, we are asking whether the writer *meant* to have all of his characters be *believable* representatives of reality. Second, we are judging the writer's ability to make his characters seem real. That we are doing these two different things, judging intention and skill, means that we must begin our analysis by trying to determine whether or not a writer wanted his characters to seem real, or, perhaps, *which* of his characters he wanted to seem real.

Sometimes a writer deliberately exaggerates a character's personality in order to dramatize his qualities. In the exaggeration we discover a departure from reality, and the character is not entirely believable—though he is perhaps just as meaningful. Many characters are developed from the vantage point of fantasy rather than that of realism, and thus we must be sure of the author's apparent attention before evaluating the success of his characterization. Credibility is generally considered a virtue in fiction, because we like to feel that characters are real, are people we might actually meet. If it is obvious that an author is trying to make a character believable and the character is definitely unbelievable, we must regard it as an artistic failure.

MOTIVATION. The nature of characters in fiction, like that of characters in drama, is revealed through action, dialogue, and description. These three methods of characterization all relate, in different ways and with varying intensity, to considerations of motivation. As students writing about literature we need to ask *why* a character says what he does and acts the ways he does. Characters, as people, are the way they are and do the things they do for reasons, even though these reasons are not necessarily apparent to *them*. People, and therefore characters, have desires and frustrations, and in their individual ways they try to maximize the fulfillment of their desires and minimize their frustrations. Psychologists tell us that the fear of punishment and the hope of reward are the two main motivations (and, in a way, they are also the same) behind all people, but the various combinations and patterns of behavior slant toward those simple motives with only marginal clarity. Motivation is not always easy to discover, but it *is* there, and the author puts it there, and thus in analyzing fiction we must always attempt to come to grips with it. *Round* characters, and indeed most *major* characters, are developed to some extent in terms of their motives. An author may be more successful in portraying one character's motives than those of another, and usually certain characters' actions are so consistent with what we sense about their nature that we think of them as *convincing* (not simply as credible). Some characters are not extensively developed in terms of motivation—though some such development is essential—and in these cases we tend to regard the characters more in terms of exposition of a particular plot rather than in terms of exposition of personality.

A work of fiction generally has more relationships than characters, for as characters come together their personalities interact and their motives, through patterns of interaction, become clear (sometimes quickly, sometimes gradually). A character's motives are generally connected to *goals;* that is, characters behave in certain ways in order to arrive at their goals.

AGE AND ENVIRONMENT. (The student should first read the discussions of *realism* and *naturalism* in the drama, pp. 145ff.)

Characters dwell in particular fictional worlds which are usually modeled on reality. Because of this we may write about characters as "products of their age and environment." Hemingway's expatriates are in many ways characteristic or typical of artistically inclined Americans living abroad, and Dickens' poor people are representative of the industrial poor of England in the 1840s. It is important to write about characters in the context of their age and surroundings, because these explain them in very basic ways. Characters, in other words, cannot be mechanically detached from their environment and discussed exclusively (or "clinically") in terms of psychological make-up. The fictional worlds which they inhabit inform them, determine them, and thus constantly qualify them. In longer fictional works authors have time to develop with considerable care the relationship between characters and their environment, while short stories may have to rely economically on a series of suggestive details to convey the sense of the reality of which they are meant to be a part.

The adolescents in Knowles' *A Separate Peace* are adolescents in a particular moment in history when scenes of Americans fighting abroad and of bombings in Central Europe are being shown every day on the newsreels at neighborhood movie houses. The boys are living in a time of national preoccupation with "the war effort," and this preoccupation has basic effects on them. Each boy, for example, must search within himself to measure his personal courage or fear and to determine how he feels about actually fighting in the war. Being sixteen years of age, each must prepare for his coming military call-up. None suspect that the war is suddenly going to end.

The characters in Hawthorne's *The Scarlet Letter* are all seen as being influenced, and in different ways directed, by a tough-minded New England Calvinism and the accompanying reality of damnation. The strict Puritan code supported by the society has untold effects on Hester while at the same time it dramatically informs the characterization of Chillingsworth.

In Fitzgerald's *The Great Gatsby* we are made acutely aware of the influence of the wealthy environment of East Egg, and of the narrator's home in West Egg. The luxurious living of the wealthy Long Island community becomes an important aspect of Gatsby's characterization.

Characters reflect their background and environment in such striking ways that the novelist often uses their backgrounds to present *dramatic contrasts*. A good example is Henry James' opening description of the gawky, uncivilized title character of *The American;* here we are introduced to the representative self-made American businessman with no sense of propriety and fashion sitting in an elegant European museum in the middle of the nineteenth century:

> On a brilliant day in May, in the year 1868, a gentleman was reclining at his ease on the great circular divan which at that period occupied the centre of the Salon Carré, in the Museum of the Louvre. This commodious ottoman has since been removed, to the extreme regret of all weak-kneed lovers of the fine arts, but the gentleman in question had taken serene possession of its softest spot, and, with his head thrown back and his legs outstretched, was staring at Murillo's beautiful moon-borne Madonna in profound enjoyment of his posture.

James' American is sitting in a comfortable, sprawling manner—the completely wrong way to sit on a divan in the Louvre! He likes being comfortable. He is enjoying his posture, not the painting. This characterizes him a great deal. The reader is immediately sensitive to the American's lack of understanding of what is "proper." This is his distinctly nouveau-riche American heritage. Throughout the novel James develops a sharp contrast between the typically refined European's *savoir-faire* and the embarrassingly insensitive and unrefined behavior of the American living abroad who is, as it were, "doing the arts." James' American has come to Europe to be broadened. He is innocently unaware of the nature of good taste and decorum and thus he is very happy to have his legs sprawled out gawkily as he relaxes comfortably on a divan in the Louvre. James' character is very much a product of his environment—and he will meet characters who are very much products of theirs. The characters will become dramatically interlocked through their differences in background.

A novelist may describe characters' backgrounds directly. Or, he may allow their backgrounds to be revealed gradually through their words and actions (though usually both means are used in order to broaden the characterization). The relationship between characters and their environments, furthermore, is a two-way street in terms of the novelist's art. Just as a novelist uses revelation of background to develop his characters, so too he uses his characters to reveal their background. Dickens' characters are products of an age, of a time and place in the development of industrial England, and their environment explains them. But the characters also explain their environment. In Little Jo (*Bleak House*) we find Dickens' portrait of a very poor child who has been wronged by society; however, the portrait tells us more about that society than it tells us about him. Little Jo may be felt as a kind of "mirror to society." In him we see what is wrong with his environment. The idea of holding up a mirror to life is as old as literature. In characters we may, then, discover a writer's feelings of love, scorn, distrust, and hatred of various features of the real world.

Setting

In discussing the relationship between characters and their environment we have, really, been approaching the subject of setting (James' Europe in 1868, Dickens' England in the 1840s, and so forth). But we have been thinking in terms of the *overall setting*, a time and place in history, and not, really, in terms of *particular setting*. Knowles' *A Separate Peace* could be taking place at any private boys' school during the later years of America's involvement in World War II. But the point is that it takes place at the Devon School, and that Devon is meant to be a prototype of the New England prep school. The particular setting, then, is informed by all of our conventional associations with New England and with the peaceful, undisturbed, orderly tranquility of life at a quiet, prosperous school for boys (Exeter, Andover, etc.). Consider one of the Knowles' comments about Devon:

> Devon is sometimes considered the most beautiful school in New England, and even on this dismal afternoon its power was asserted. It is the beauty of small areas of order—a large yard, a group of trees, three similar dormitories, a circle of old houses —living together in contentious harmony.

Knowles goes on to describe the old colonial houses and the campus atmosphere which will play a large part in the exposition of the central story. The contrast between the tradition and tranquility of a typical, traditional small New England school and the enormous suffocating national war effort on the outside forms a dramatic contrast and thereby generates dramatic qualities like tension and conflict.

When writing about the setting of a work of fiction a student should mention the specific characteristics of the period in which the story is taking place. He should also describe some of the particulars of the setting and the bearing which they have on the plot and the characters. While some *poems* may be discussed without consideration of historical period, most works of prose fiction have settings in history (time, place) which are extremely important to the overall meaning. The period of time which the work of fiction covers is a large consideration; our comments about *A Separate Peace, The Scarlet Letter,* and *The Great Gatsby* should make this clear. However, a work of fiction transcends its setting. While some qualities of a novel are bound up with the society which it reflects, other qualities have a "universality" about them. The reader, then, needs constantly to try to separate those qualities which connect to the period and particulars of the setting from those which have implications for all men in all times and places. Some of the characters' *assumptions* will reflect the fact that they are living at a certain time in a certain place, but others will instead reflect their essential humanity or individual psychological make-up. A man who is fiercely jealous in a novel set in Victorian England has certain things in common with a man who is fiercely jealous in a novel set in New York in the 1970s. Detail, style, assumptions, actions, and other areas of consideration all must, then, be approached with an understanding of the separateness of the particular setting and the universality of certain human emotions and attitudes.

It should be pointed out, finally, that setting is often used in a symbolic manner. The fog which menacingly smothers everything in the opening of Dickens' *Bleak House* is meant to symbolize the choking, suffocating inertia of Chancery law cases which drag on indefinitely. The symbolic nature of the fog is so obvious that some critics have attacked Dickens' lack of subtlety and written that his symbols are simply hung out over the door so that the reader cannot possibly miss them. Dickens tells us that "At the very heart of the fog, sits the Lord High Chancellor in his High Court of Chancery." The equation is immediate, simple, and complete.

A writer of fiction often describes the setting in such a way that the symbolic overtones cannot be missed; this is particularly true of Hardy's landscapes. Consider his discussion of the Vale of Blackmoor in *Tess of the D'Urbervilles* in which the delicate and fertile quality of the landscape is introduced to prepare us for the forthcoming story:

> Here, in the valley, the world seems to be constructed upon a smaller and more delicate scale; the fields are mere paddocks, so reduced that from this height their hedgerows appear a network of dark green threads overspreading the paler green of the grass. The atmosphere beneath is languorous, and is so tinged with azure that what artists call the middle partakes also of that hue, while the horizon beyond is of the deepest ultramarine. Arable lands are few and limited; with but slight exceptions the prospect is a broad rich mass of grass and trees . . .

The richness, lushness, and greenness will be mentioned frequently as a kind of symbolic context behind Tess' seduction. In order to foreshadow the significance of this setting, Hardy goes on to comment in a manner that self-consciously lends mythic qualities to the setting:

> The district is of historic, no less than of topographical interest. The Vale was known in former times as the Forest of White Hart, from a curious legend of King Henry III's reign, in which the killing by a certain Thomas de la Lynd of a beau-

> tiful white hart which the king had run down and spared, was made the occasion of a heavy fine.

This kind of deliberate amplifying of the associations of the setting is in the mainstream of artistic symbolism in fiction, and we meet it again and again. This leads us to considerations of style.

Style

When we examine a fiction writer's *style* we are, essentially, considering his *diction*—the kinds of words he uses to describe characters, action, and setting—his *imagery* (see earlier discussions of imagery in the poetry and drama sections, pp. 42ff., 105ff.), his sentence structure, or syntax, and his handling of *dialogue.*

Because the prose style of a particular work tends to be relatively uniform, diction is relatively simple to examine. Some writers prefer using numerous qualifying adverbs and adjectives, while others tend to rely primarily on strong verbs. Diction, the choice of words, is bound up with both imagery and sentence structure. Short crisp sentences tend to exclude any heavy adverbial quality, while long, flowing sentences with numerous clauses tend to contain numerous adverbs and adjectives. A fiction writer's diction evolves from certain artistic decisions—to use colloquial language rather than formal language, to use familiar words rather than strange words, to use more literal than figurative language, to phrase ideas economically or to develop them in longer, flowing sentences, and so forth.

Hemingway is a fiction writer who tends to write simple, direct sentences. He relies on strong verbs of action and thus his writing tends to record physical acts—the doing—rather than the cerebral anguish accompanying those acts. Hemingway's style is self-consciously sparse, almost staccato-like in its directness; consider, for example, this short passage from *The Sun Also Rises:*

> I do not know what time I got to bed. I remember undressing, putting on a bathrobe, and standing out on the balcony. I knew

> I was quite drunk, and when I came in I put on the light over the head of the bed and started to read. I was reading a book by Turgenieff. Probably I read the same page over several times. It was one of the stories in "A Sportsman's Sketches." I had read it before, but it seemed quite new. The country became very clear and the feeling of pressure in my head seemed to loosen. I was very drunk and I did not want to shut my eyes because the room would go round and round. If I kept on reading that feeling would pass.

This narration has a solid realism. We know exactly how the narrator feels. We do not mind the repetition of the same simple sentence structure—"I did this, I did that, etc."—because we feel that the style has a basic honesty about it. The diction is unpretentious and direct. There are no unfamiliar words. There are no lengthy sentences. Emphasis is on the verbs which are used primarily to carry the story forward and to deepen our feeling for the narrator.

Now let us reexamine the opening passage of Henry James' *The American.* Notice the unusual words—the diction is more ornate than Hemingway's—and the complicated sentence structure:

> On a brilliant day in May, in the year 1868, a gentleman was reclining at his ease on the great circular divan which at that period occupied the centre of the Salon Carré, in the Museum of the Louvre. This commodious ottoman has since been removed, to the extreme regret of all weak-kneed lovers of the fine arts, but the gentleman in question had taken serene possession of its softest spot, and, with his head thrown back and his legs outstretched, was staring at Murillo's beautiful moon-borne Madonna in profound enjoyment of his posture.

Notice that James uses adjectives abundantly, and the unusually long second sentence piles up qualifying clauses. Hemingway would simply say that someone sits on a couch and throws his legs out; James, however, tells us that someone is taking "serene possession" of the softest spot of the divan! Hemingway might say that his character is comfortable, while James writes that his

American is "in profound enjoyment of his posture"! Hemingway and James represent extremes; one employs diction and sentence structure which are unusually simple, while the other employs diction and sentence structure which are unusually complex. Most writers of fiction lean toward one extreme or the other. The important thing is not really to decide whether a particular writer is more like James or more like Hemingway, but rather simply to notice the way his style *works:* if he uses simple diction, what is the effect? If he uses complex sentences, do they advance the reader's intimacy with the setting, or his feeling for the atmosphere of the particular fictional world?

While I have asserted that simplicity of diction and simplicity of syntax often go together, there is absolutely no reason why they need to, and many times they do not. It is altogether possible to have elaborate diction and simple direct sentences, or simple diction and more elaborate sentence structure. Consider the latter combination in the following passage from James Baldwin's *Go Tell It on the Mountain:*

> The silence in the church ended when Brother Elisha, kneeling near the piano, cried out and fell backward under the power of the Lord. Immediately, two or three others cried out also, and a wind, a foretaste of that great downpouring they awaited, swept the church. With this cry, and the echoing cries, the tarry service moved from its first stage of steady murmuring, broken by moans and now and again an isolated cry, into that stage of tears and groaning, of calling aloud and singing, which was like the labor of a woman about to be delivered of her child. On this threshing-floor the child was the soul that struggled to the light, and it was the church that was in labor, that did not cease to push and pull, calling out the name of Jesus.

The dramatic analogy between the church's labor and that of a woman giving birth is not particularly unusual though it *is* striking; the diction is familiar and descriptive without being at all excessive. The sentences, however, are simple. Baldwin is very movingly picturing an emotional revival session in a Harlem church. As an artist he is aware of the danger of elevating his language beyond the typicality and familiarity of the scene.

Imagery in prose is quite common. A writer tries to use certain words at certain times in order to make the reader associate certain characters or places with certain qualities. Novels—like poems and plays—have certain *patterns of imagery* which the reader discovers by examining the diction and, specifically, the descriptive words which are repeated. When images are repeated frequently enough they sometimes become *symbols* (see the discussion of imagery in the poetry section, pp. 42ff.). In Dickens' *Bleak House* there is the pattern of fog imagery which continuously reminds us of the horribly muddled nature of the Chancery law courts. Also, every character in the book is slowly associated either with beasts (and birds) of prey, or with beasts and birds which are preyed upon.

Imagery is part of style and a writer's metaphors bear strongly upon the overall *meaning* of his story. Imagery is connected to diction, because a writer is usually deciding to be either more figurative—using many metaphors and similes—or more literal—using very few metaphors and similes. Hemingway is literal, and he tells his story directly. Dickens is figurative and tries to dramatize his story by introducing a large number of metaphors and similes which, taken together, form the main patterns of imagery.

Images are used most frequently to introduce, artistically, sensory experience into the narrative. Images are used to present vivid descriptions of sensory experience; we see a striking example of this use of imagery in the opening of Joyce's sophisticated autobiographical novel, *A Portrait of the Artist as a Young Man.* This opening is presented from a child's point of view; the fairy-tale motif of the first sentence suggests the coming of age of the prince of art, and then introduces images which relate to sensory experience—of smell, of hot and cold, of color:

> Once upon a time and a very good time it was there was a moocow coming down along the road and this moocow that was coming down along the road met a nicens little boy named baby tuckoo. . . .
>
> His father told him that story: his father looked at him through a glass: he had a hairy face.
>
> He was baby tuckoo. The moocow came down the road where Betty Byrne lived: she sold lemon platt.

O, the wild rose blossoms
On the little green place.

He sang that song. That was his song.

O, the green wothe botheth.

When you wet the bed, first it is warm then it gets cold. His mother put on the oilsheet. That had the queer smell.

His mother had a nicer smell than his father. She played on the piano the sailor's hornpipe for him to dance. He danced:

Tralala lala
Tralala tralaladdy,
Tralala lala,
Tralala lala.

Uncle Charles and Dante clapped. They were older than his father and mother but Uncle Charles was older than Dante.

Dante had two brushes in her press. The brush with the maroon velvet back was for Michael Davitt and the brush with the green velvet back was for Parnell. Dante gave him a cachou every time he brought her a piece of tissue paper.

Joyce's evocation of particular sensations vividly presents us with the world seen and experienced by the child (a world Joyce will frequently return to), while at the same time preparing us for recurrent associations between green and Irish nationalism ("Parnell").

While a fiction writer's style is often most distinctive when he is writing *description,* the handling of *dialogue* also forms part of his style. As an artist, he must, first of all, make his characters speak in a manner and tone which is appropriate to their backgrounds, personalities, and social positions. Some characters speak in a formal way and some speak in a more colloquial manner. The content of dialogue is subject to considerable artistic manipulation, and thus we must devote careful attention to it. And a writer must decide whether to make the dialogue consist primarily of short statements. Writing particular *dialects* also demands artistic control.

We also need to notice the ways in which a writer qualifies characters' dialogue. Sometimes we find simply a series of "he said" and "she said"; sometimes there are direct adverbial qualifiers—"he said gingerly," "she said angrily," and so forth. And sometimes a writer simply stops the dialogue to tell us, in a sentence or more, precisely how a person is speaking. Consider the movement of the dialogue in a story by Joyce:

> "How much is a plate of peas?" he asked.
> "Three halfpence, sir," said the girl.
> "Bring me a plate of peas," he said, "and a bottle of ginger beer."
> He spoke roughly in order to belie his air of gentility for his entry had been followed by a pause of talk.

The "asked-said-said" pattern shifts when Joyce stops to qualify with the sentence "He spoke roughly." Generally, a fiction writer tries to mix the patterns he uses to present dialogue, relying heavily on the direct form of "he said," but also using stylistic variation through adverbs, interruptions, and, sometimes, colons. Consider another dialogue by Joyce:

> The smile passed away from Gabriel's face. A dull anger began to gather at the back of his mind and the dull fires of his lust began to grow angrily in his veins.
> "Someone you were in love with?" he asked ironically.
> "It was a young boy I used to know," she answered, "named Michael Furey. He used to sing that song, *The Lass of Aughrim*. He was very delicate."
> Gabriel was silent. He did not wish her to think that he was interested in this delicate boy.
> "I can see him so plainly," she said, after a moment. "Such eyes as he had: big, dark eyes! And such an expression in them—an expression!"
> "O, then you were in love with him?" said Gabriel.
> "I used to go out walking with him," she said, "when I was in Galway."
> A thought flew across Gabriel's mind.
> "Perhaps that was why you wanted to go to Galway with that Ivors girl?" he said coldly.
> She looked at him and asked in surprise:
> "What for?"

> Her eyes made Gabriel feel awkward. He shrugged his shoulders and said:
>
> "How do I know? To see him, perhaps."
>
> She looked away from him along the shaft of light towards the window in silence.
>
> "He is dead," she said at length. "He died when he was only seventeen. Isn't it a terrible thing to die so young as that?"
>
> "What was he?" asked Gabriel, still ironically.
>
> "He was in the gasworks," she said.
>
> Gabriel felt humiliated by the failure of his irony and by the evocation of this figure from the dead, a boy in the gasworks.

In presenting this dialogue from his famous story "The Dead" in *Dubliners,* Joyce has used a great variety of artistic methods. The movement of "he asked ironically" to "asked Gabriel, still ironically" to the final comment on "the failure of his irony" is carefully planned. The conversation is sophisticated, and yet natural and understandable. Sometimes an adverb—"ironically" or "coldly"—follows the verb; sometimes a colon introduces the statement and thus gives the dialogue a swift, dramatic movement. When writing about an author's style, then, and focusing on his diction, sentence structure, and imagery, the student should also pay attention to the subtle variations in presenting dialogue which makes fiction writers highly individualistic. Some writers omit verbs, some omit punctuation marks, some rely extensively on one manner of presenting dialogue more than another (and all introduce diction designed to form part of the characterization).

A few other considerations must be made in connection with style. The first is the balance—or ratio or proportion—between narration and dialogue. Is there more of one than the other, and, if so, why? Does the writer handle narration more artistically than he handles dialogue? Does the dialogue characterize as successfully as the description? In short, the student must examine the relationship, within the work of fiction, between narration and dialogue in order to make some comment on the writer's art.

Secondly, we can ask if there are any *peculiarities of style.* Does the writer omit a great deal of basic punctuation or alter the format of conventional English sentence structure? Does he rely extensively on particular parts of speech such as adverbs or verbs? Is there a pedantry about his diction?

And, lastly, we need to consider whether a writer's style in any way *interferes* with the advancement of the story. Because a writer is trying to entertain his reader he may choose to put the lion's share of his creative energy into stylistic entertainment rather than into the narration of an actual story. In the more sophisticated writers, of course, both style and story are engaging. The balance, or relationship, between story-telling and stylistic considerations is inherently bound up with the writer's purpose.

The Meaning of Fiction

We have been thinking, up until this point, primarily about the ingredients of fiction in terms of formalistic analysis. What hangs like an open umbrella over all considerations of structure, characterization, and style, however, is *meaning*. Fiction deals with experience, either real or imagined. Characters have definite feelings about what happens to them, and, by revealing characters' feelings, an author gives us much of the meaning of his work.

In fiction, as we have suggested, there is a "reality" which may or may not correspond to the reality which we, as readers, perceive. But characters in fictional worlds react to what is reality *for them*. To interpret fiction, it follows, we must see characters in terms of *their* perception of their experience, and then determine the author's intention in recording particular kinds of perception. Sometimes we are able to define—through characters' perception of experiences—the author's attitude toward man, life, nature, and so forth. The author's attitude, in turn, directs us to the heart of the meaning of his works. While we need to understand the artistic principles of the *craft* of fiction, then, we must nevertheless remember that when we write about fiction we are, above all else, trying to record meaning. Novels and stories achieve very particular *effects*, because they *mean* in very particular ways. We only *know* a work of fiction when we know what it *means*.

In determining essential meaning, we must do more than study the way characters feel about what happens to them (though this *is* the safest starting point). We need to ask whether an author is making certain *assumptions* about the world he is creating. Then, too, we need to differentiate clearly between an author's *unconscious* assumptions and those assumptions which become clearly stated ideas. What importance for the meaning is there in the author's initial selection of a specific point of view? What are the stylistic effects as they bear on meaning? We need, further, to realize that a fictional work may have one, total meaning —without having every part of the work supporting it. Which episodes seem to have the most importance? Does the collective experience of the main characters "add up" to any *one* meaning at all? Does the author retreat into intentional ambiguity?

The meaning of fiction, and therefore writing *about* fiction, also involves the student in *classification*. First, the work of fiction must be classified by way of genre: science fiction *means* in a way different from historical fiction. Secondly, classification as to "levels of meaning" must be made: is the work's basic meaning apparent at the level of story (plot), or is it substantially apparent at the level of implication and analogy? (The societies visited by Swift's Gulliver have their meaning by way of reference to English society.) Finally, we need to classify fiction according to the author's *emphasis*. Is the story to be read *primarily* in terms of events? of personalities? of environmental forces? What aspect of the work seems to receive the greatest part of the author's attention and artistic effort?

The classification of fiction, in short, demands that the reader be sensitive to both the author's overt emphasis and to the larger literary tradition from which the work borrows. Is it a *realistic* fictional work, holding up a mirror to life as it is? Is it naturalistic, attempting to explain *why* life is as it is in terms of behavioral, historical, psychological, or environmental forces? (See the discussion of *realism* and *naturalism* in the drama section, pp. 145ff.) By focusing on the *experience* and the classification of a particular work, then, we are able to reach conclusions about meaning.

The Judgment of Fiction

When we have a sound understanding of the author's handling of event, character, and story, a general appreciation of matters of style, and a grasp of primary meaning, our final and all-important endeavor must be to *judge*. Has the author *successfully* conveyed meaning? Has he achieved his intended purpose? Is it evident that he has had control over his materials?

Perhaps the best way to order one's judgment of fictional works is to think in terms of Goethe's famous three questions: (1) What is the work trying to do? (2) Does it succeed? (3) Was it worth doing? It is perhaps in answering the third question that the student must exercise the greatest discrimination. Above all, one must be sure to differentiate *moral* judgment from *aesthetic* judgment. Many readers of Joyce's *Ulysses* had a mixed judgment, for example, for they felt the novel to be an *artistic* success, but nevertheless not *morally* defensible (most recent Joyce criticism has reversed that second view). Finally, because fiction is so varied in kind, the judgment of fiction demands measuring the degree of a writer's innovation. It may be concluded that a writer's experimentalism in itself may be praiseworthy, even though the particular work under consideration may not be the total or ideal fulfillment (application) of the experimental idea *behind* the work. In any case, the student must, in the end, form an opinion, an estimate, a conclusion about the value of a fictional work. This final judgment transcends matters of "schools of criticism" (social, psychological, formalist, etc.) and is symbolic of the artist's granting of freedom to his individual readers to make up their own minds about what he has written.

Index